WE WILL SING!

Simple Gifts
© Copyright 1950 by Aaron Copland. Copyright Renewed.
Used by permission of the Aaron Copland Fund for Music, Inc., Copyright owner.
Sole Publisher and Licensee, Boosey & Hawkes, Inc.

Ching-a-ring Chaw
© Copyright 1954 by Aaron Copland. Copyright Renewed.
Used by permission of the Aaron Copland Fund for Music, Inc., Copyright owner.
Sole Publisher and Licensee, Boosey & Hawkes, Inc.

The following works are used by permission:

The Sally Gardens
© Copyright 1943 Boosey & Co., Ltd. Copyright Renewed.

She's Like the Swallow
© Copyright 1992 by Boosey & Hawkes, Inc.

A Spring Morning
© Copyright 1993 by Boosey & Hawkes, Inc.

The Path to the Moon
© Copyright 1956 by Boosey & Co. Ltd.; Copyright Renewed.

Oliver Cromwell
© Copyright 1943 by Boosey & Co. Ltd.; Copyright Renewed.

Bist du bei mir
© Copyright 1993 by Boosey & Hawkes, Inc.

"Hodie" from A Ceremony of Carols
© Copyright 1943 by Boosey & Co. Ltd.; Copyright Renewed.

Jingle Bell Swing
© Copyright 1992 by Boosey & Hawkes, Inc.

Kodály-Curwen Handsigns
from SIGHT AND SOUND by Arpad Darazs and Stephen Jay
© Copyright 1965 by Boosey & Hawkes, Inc.; Copyright Renewed.

Cassette Symbol
© Copyright by New Vision Technologies, Inc.

Contributing Editors: Anne L. Schelleng, John Forbes

Book Design: Mirror Mountain Productions

Cover Design: Russell Stretten Design, London NW1

Photography: Jim Steere; Cover Photography: Steven Laschever

Problem solving exercise sheets are available as reproducible black-line masters in the
WE WILL SING! Resource Pack (TXB 82).

WE WILL SING!

Choral Music Experience for Classroom Choirs

by Doreen Rao

Assisting Authors:

Lori-Anne Dolloff

Sandra Prodan

Boosey & Hawkes
New York • London • Toronto • Bonn • Sydney • Tokyo

In memory of Doreen Merritt (1923-1990), a truly beautiful singer, and Harvey Ringel (1903-1992), her singing teacher and mine.

Well, there are colleagues and then there are colleagues.

When the Hungarian composer and music educator Zoltán Kodály says, "Music belongs to everyone" and the Russian Dmitri Kabalevsky, "Every class should be a choir", they give us a vision which is most challenging – but not impossible to achieve. Some of us, their successors as musicians and educators, have courageously set out to cut the road towards that goal.

Doreen Rao, my American colleague, has created a new version for her Choral Music Experience project. We Will Sing! is a message to all music educators and to our students all over the world. With a great artistic and pedagogic professionality and human warmth, she has realized the road "to develop musicianship, to enjoy the opportunities to perform great music, and to participate in world culture through singing."

I warmly recommend it to classrooms, community choirs, and across borders.

Erkki Pohjola
Conductor, Tapiola Choir
Tapiola, Finland
August, 1993

Table of Contents

Acknowledgements ix
Preface xi

PART 1 Invitation to Choral Music Experience 1

We Will Sing! At a Glance 3
    Part 1 Invitation to CME for Classroom Choirs 3
    Part 2 Singing 4
    Part 3 Singing with Musicianship 4
    Part 4 Singing Together 5
        Performance Projects 5
        Orientations 5
        Rehearsal Guides 5
        Reflecting and Evaluating 6
        Selected Recordings 6

Invitation to Choral Music Experience for Classroom Choirs
for the Teacher-Conductor 7
    Principles of Music Performance as Music Education 7
    The Aims of Music Performance 7
    A Curriculum for Classroom Choirs 7
    Instructional Methods for Classroom Choirs 8
    The Role of the Teacher-Conductor 8
    The Role of the Student 9
    A Teaching Model for Classroom Choirs 9
    Assessment Alternatives for Classroom Choirs 10

Invitation to Choral Music Experience for Classroom Choirs
for the Student 11
    How can I develop my musical potential? 11
    What will I learn through music performance? 11
    How will I develop my musicianship? 11
    What are the requirements in music performance? 12
    How can my teacher help me? 12
    How will I be assessed in my music performance program? 12
        Performance Portfolio 13

PART 2 Singing 15

Practice Project One: Your Singing Voice 17
Describe Your First Performance 17
Using Your Voice as a Musical Instrument 17
Listening to Vocal Artists 18
You and Your Singing Voice 18
Summary 19
    Selected Recordings 19
    Performance Portfolio 20

Practice Project Two: Finding Your Singing Voice 21
Ways of Using Your Voice 21
The Stage Voice 21
Your Speaking Voice 21
Comparing Speaking and Singing 22
Using Your Own Voice 22
Speech Patterns 22
Vocal Range 23
Summary 23
    Performance Portfolio 24

Practice Project Three: Exercising Your Singing Voice 25
Exercise 25
Posture 26
Breathing 27
Tone Production 28
Summary 30
    Selected Recordings 30
    Performance Portfolio 24

Practice Project Four: Using Your Singing Voice 33
Shaping the Vowel 33
Vocal Diction 34
International Phonetic Alphabet 34
    Vowels 35
    Five "Basic" Singing Vowels 35
    Other Common Vowels in Singing 35
    Neutral Vowels 35
    Diphthongs 35
Vowel Modification 35
Vowel Chart Using IPA Symbols 35
Consonants 37
Using Phonetic Analysis 37

Rules for Singing r 37
Summary 37
    Selected Recordings 37
    Performance Portfolio 38

PART 3 Singing With Musicianship 39

Practice Project Five: Understanding the Score 41
Following the Score 41
    Text 41
    Vocal Line 41
    Treble Clef 41
    Bass Clef 44
    The Musical Staff 44
    Bar Line 44
    Meter Signature 44
    Measure 44
    System 44
    Key Signature 44
    Tempo Markings 44
    Dynamics 44
    Phrase Markings 45
    Articulation 45
Performance Practice 45
Interpretation 45
Summary 45
    Selected Recordings 46
    Performance Portfolio 47

Practice Project Six: Feeling Time and Reading Rhythm 49
Meter and Meter Signatures 49
Conducting Time 50
    Duple Meter 51
    Triple Meter 52
    Conducting in 4 53
Compound Meter 54
Other Meters 56
Free Meter 57
Reading Rhythm 58
    Using Words 58
    Using the Metric System 59
    Counting Rests 61
    Using Rhythm Syllables 61
Syncopation 63
Summary 65
    Performance Portfolio 66

Practice Project Seven: Hearing Pitch and Reading Notation 69

Using Tonic Solfa 70

Curwen-Kodály Handsigns 71

Major Tonality 72

Making Scales 73

At the Keyboard 73

Absolute Pitch Names 75

Finding Do 77

Minor Tonality 78

Pitch Alterations - Accidentals 78

Chromatic Syllables and Handsigns 79

Intervals 81

Major Intervals 81

Minor Intervals 82

Summary 82

Performance Portfolio 83

PART 4 Singing Together

PERFORMANCE PROJECTS Program One

PERFORMANCE PROJECTS Program One 89

O Music, Sweet Music (Mason/Rao) 90

Orientation 90

Rehearsal Guide 94

Selected Recordings 95

Performance Portfolio 96

The Sally Gardens (arr. Britten) 98

Orientation 98

Rehearsal Guide 103

Selected Recordings 104

Performance Portfolio 105

Simple Gifts (arr. Copland) 106

Orientation 106

Rehearsal Guide 109

Selected Recordings 110

Performance Portfolio 112

She's Like the Swallow (arr. Dolloff) 114
   Orientation 114
   Rehearsal Guide 120
      Selected Recordings 121
      Performance Portfolio 122

A Spring Morning (Carey/Rao) 124
   Orientation 124
   Rehearsal Guide 128
      Performance Portfolio 131

Good Night (Kabalevsky) 132
   Orientation 132
   Rehearsal Guide 136
      Selected Recordings 137
      Performance Portfolio 138

PERFORMANCE PROJECTS Program Two 139

Jubilate Deo (Praetorius/Rao) 140
   Orientation 140
   Rehearsal Guide 142
      Selected Recordings 143
      Performance Portfolio 144

The Path to the Moon (Thiman) 146
   Orientation 146
   Rehearsal Guide 150
      Selected Recordings 151
      Performance Portfolio 152

I Know Where I'm Goin' (arr. Hughes) 154
   Orientation 154
   Rehearsal Guide 157
      Selected Recordings 158
      Performance Portfolio 159

Oliver Cromwell (arr. Britten) 160
   Orientation 160
   Rehearsal guide 165
      Selected Recordings 166
      Performance Portfolio 167

Bist du bei mir (Bach) 168
   Orientation 168
   Rehearsal Guide 172
      Selected Recordings 173
      Performance Portfolio 174

Ching-a-ring Chaw (arr. Copland) 176
   Orientation 176
   Rehearsal Guide 184
      Selected Recordings 185
      Performance Portfolio 187

PERFORMANCE PROJECTS Program Three 189

"Hodie" from A Ceremony of Carols, Opus 28 (Britten) 190
   Orientation 190
   Rehearsal Guide 194
      Selected Recordings 196
      Performance Portfolio 197

A Child is Born (Anon.) 198
   Orientation 198
   Rehearsal Guide 200
      Performance Portfolio 202

Poor Little Children (Spiritual) 204
   Orientation 204
   Rehearsal Guide 206
      Selected Recordings 207
      Performance Portfolio 208

"How Beautiful are the Feet of Them" from Messiah (Handel) 210
   Orientation 210
   Rehearsal Guide 215
      Selected Recordings 216
      Performance Portfolio 217

In Dulci Jubilo (Bach) 218
   Orientation 218
   Rehearsal Guide 222
      Selected Recordings 223
      Performance Portfolio 224

Jingle Bell Swing (arr. Elliott) 226
  Orientation 226
  Rehearsal Guide 233
    Selected Recordings 234
    Performance Portfolio 235

Appendix 237

Glossary of Musical Terms 239

Resources for the Teacher-Conductor 243

PREFACE

We Will Sing! is a *performance-based* textbook for classroom students and the teachers who guide them. Auditioned choirs and community-based choral programs will find this curriculum a useful way of organizing and sequencing rehearsals at the beginning levels of choral music experience. *We Will Sing!* may also be used as a college textbook for courses in elementary music education and choral methods.

The book's title *We Will Sing!* is a quotation from Lowell Mason's school song, *O Music, Sweet Music.* This familiar and historically significant tune is performed regularly by the Glen Ellyn Children's Chorus as a *choir favorite.* I have chosen the book's title and Lowell Mason's school song for this textbook in an effort to encourage choral singing in the classroom, a tradition at the heart of music education.

We Will Sing! is a multicultural effort. It begins with the contemporary music of the United States, Canada, and England. It is augmented with the European classics of Bach, Handel, and Praetorius. And it includes traditional Russian and Irish folk songs as well as Negro spirituals and jazz. Such a distinctive and diverse repertoire is the first step in giving students the opportunity to participate in culture.

In the past, music education has viewed "musical understanding" as something different from musical performing. Today we know that when students perform musically, they are *demonstrating their knowledge* – they are *singing their understanding.* The ability to sing in a choir counts as a form of knowledge. This kind of *thinking-in-action* insures our students the opportunity to learn more about themselves and more about the world around them.

Few would deny that musical enjoyment and self-growth is the bottom line for music education today. Children do not develop musically by dabbling in the "arts" or by engaging in a series of unrelated "activities." Just *doing something* is not enough. In music education, musical enjoyment and self-growth develops from the ability to produce music, to perform music with skill and understanding, to meet the musical challenges with musicianship, and to take command of the musical materials. Musical enjoyment and self-growth comes from *doing something well!*

A *revolution from within* music education begins by insuring that all children have the opportunity to *produce* music with the singing voice, *practice* musicianship, and *perform* great music with skill and understanding. As music educators learn to trust the democratic ideals of excellence, we will again view choral singing as something worth doing for its own sake. Performance challenges children to improve – to transcend the ordinary in favor of something superior. Music is like culture. It is not something people have – it is something people *do!*

It is my hope that *We Will Sing! Choral Music Experience for Classroom Choirs* empowers your students to develop musicianship, to enjoy the opportunities to perform great music, and to participate in world culture through singing.

© Doreen Rao, 1992

ACKNOWLEGMENTS

It is fitting that a *music* textbook should be undertaken by a *music* publisher, particularly one that has been regarded worldwide for over 150 years. Special thanks are due to Anne Schelleng and John Forbes of Boosey & Hawkes, New York for their many hours of patient work. My gratitude also extends to colleagues at Boosey & Hawkes, London whose breadth of experience and dedication to this project brought invaluable perspectives.

I am deeply grateful to my writing assistants Lori-Anne Dolloff (Canada) and Sandra Prodan (United States) who spent time, energy, and considerable expertise in carrying out writing and editorial assignments.

I wish to thank my colleagues, particularly the *CME* Associates of North America who believe that the opportunity for choral singing belongs to every child. Thank you Tim Sharp of the Dade County Public Schools for inspiring the idea of a choral textbook for classroom choirs, thank you Linda Ferreira for taking this repertoire and this approach to the children of rural Tennessee and thank you Janet Funderburk-Galvan for hours of patient and perceptive proof-reading. Finally, my thanks to David Elliott whose articulate and contemporary views give a new voice to music performance as music education.

Doreen Rao, Ph.D

Doreen Rao

Conductor and master teacher Doreen Rao is recognized as one of North America's leading authorities on music performance in music education. She is Associate Professor of Music and Director of Choral Programs at the University of Toronto where she conducts the University Symphony Chorus, the MacMillan Singers and teaches advanced choral conducting. Prior to her arrival at the University of Toronto, Doreen Rao held a dual appointment as assistant conductor of the Chicago Symphony Chorus and music director of the Glen Ellyn Children's Chorus, an outstanding music performance program recognized as a model for American music education and acclaimed for its award winning recordings with the Chicago Symphony Orchestra. During her long association with the Chicago Symphony Orchestra and Chorus, Doreen Rao helped prepare recorded performances that won four Grammy Awards and a Grand Prix du Disque under Margaret Hillis, Sir Georg Solti and James Levine. She has appeared extensively as guest conductor and choral clinician throughout the world. A CBS television documentary called Doreen Rao's musical achievements "extraordinary."

Regarded internationally for her commitment to children's choirs, Dr. Rao founded the ACDA National Committee on Children's Choirs and chaired the Committee for nearly ten years. She is the author of the Doreen Rao *Choral Music Experience* series of music and books published by Boosey & Hawkes, New York and Director of the CME Institute for Choral Teacher Education. Dr. Rao has been honored by the YWCA as "Outstanding Leader in Arts and Culture" and by her colleagues of the American Choral Director's Association for "Her Commitment to Choral Excellence." She is a graduate of the University of Illinois and Northwestern University where she earned a Ph.D. in Music Education.

Lori-Anne Dolloff

Lori-Anne Dolloff holds a Master's degree in music education from the University of Toronto. She has taught music at pre-school, elementary, and middle school levels, and is the director of the Mississauga Festival Choir. Mrs. Dolloff also holds a Licentiate in Organ Performance from Trinity College, London. Currently Mrs. Dolloff is an instructor at the Faculty of Music, University of Toronto, where she teaches elementary music education. An active clinician and adjudicator, Lori-Anne Dolloff holds the Artist-Teacher Diploma from Doreen Rao's Institute for Choral Teacher Education. She is completing a Ph.D. at the Ontario Institute for Studies in Education.

Sandra Prodan

Sandra Prodan received undergraduate and graduate degrees in choral music education from the University of North Carolina at Greensboro. She founded the Carolina Children's Chorus, and subsequently assumed the position of Music Director of the Glen Ellyn Children's Chorus. Under her direction, the chorus appeared at Orchestra Hall, Carnegie Hall, and at the Ravinia Festival. In addition, the GECC toured domestically and internationally, releasing two recordings.

A frequent clinician for workshops and festivals, Ms. Prodan was awarded the Artist-Teacher Diploma from Doreen Rao's Institute for Choral Teacher Education. She is on the summer faculty at the Hartt School of Music and has joined the staff of the CME Institute for Choral Teacher Education at Northern Illinois University. She is an active member of the Music Educator's National Conference and the American Choral Director's Association.

Currently, Ms. Prodan is teaching elementary music education and pursuing a Ph.D. in Music Education in Cleveland, Ohio.

PART 1

Invitation to Choral Music Experience

We Will Sing! At a Glance
A Guided Resource for Teaching and Learning

We Will Sing! is a music textbook inspired by classroom teachers and music specialists who sought quality choral music for classroom teaching and learning.

In *We Will Sing!* the students are continuously engaged in music making, or what we call *thinking-in-action.* The opportunity for students to reflect on their actions, to decide on their musical interpretation, and to evaluate the quality of their performance distinguishes *We Will Sing!* as a uniquely contemporary and progressive textbook. *Choral Music Experience for Classroom Choirs* empowers students to develop musicianship and to participate in authentic musical activity.

We Will Sing! is organized around versatile performance projects that serve the goals of school and community music programs in a variety of ways. For example: (1) the textbook can be used in its entirety as a performance-based music curriculum for classroom teaching and learning; (2) the music alone can be used in part or whole as a concert program for school or public performances; (3) the contents may be used as both a music curriculum and concert programming resource. With the aid of audio instruction and photo illustration, students can work in small groups or independently.

We Will Sing! is a music textbook that does not include a separate teaching manual. Dependency on teacher manuals or textbooks alone can make music learning artificial and often unmusical! Authentic musical activity derived from the opportunity to perform real music and solve real musical problems is the only way children gain access to a legitimate musical practice. Music teaching and learning is necessarily context dependent. *We Will Sing!* guides the teaching-learning process, encouraging each instructor to exercise individual expertise and imagination. No one should tell another expert precisely

what to do, or how to do it. At the very most, a classroom music textbook can be a guided teaching-learning resource.

Part 1 Invitation to CME for Classroom Choirs

For teachers and students, Part 1 introduces *We Will Sing!* as an opportunity to develop innate musical potential through choral music experience. Teachers are invited to learn more about the principles of curriculum and instruction underlying the music performance approach to music education. Written in a question and answer format, Part 1 also establishes a personal dialogue and collaborative spirit between students, teachers, and the book's author. Questions like *How can you develop your musical potential? What will you learn through music performance?* and *How will you develop your musicianship?* provide both students and teachers insight into the choral music experience as a unique and effective way of achieving enjoyment and self-growth.

Part 2 Singing

Part 2 begins with the performance of Lowell Mason's famous song *O Music, Sweet Music.* From that musically specific context, four practice projects provide a structured way of engaging students in the development of their singing voices, a skill central to the musical education of every child. The Practice Projects in Part 2 are not intended as isolated one-time lessons in vocal production. The exercises are designed to be utilized throughout instruction in every teaching-learning context. The vocal development of children is inextricably linked to each and every performance experience.

Project One: "Your Singing Voice" teaches children how to think about their own voices as musical instruments, and how to distinguish between singing and speaking. **Project Two: "Finding Your Singing Voice"** compares and contrasts the singing voice with the speaking voice. Through performance activities, the children experiment with different ways of using their voices for ordinary speech and for artistic expression. **Project Three: "Exercising Your Singing Voice"** gives students the opportunity to develop the vocal skills necessary to perform and enjoy singing. A sequenced series of vocal production exercises includes: (1) warm-up exercises; (2) posture models; (3) breath management directions; and (4) tone-production vocalizations. This section of vocal instruction is enhanced by photographic illustrations, and the accompanying *We Will Sing!* cassette tape. The Glen Ellyn Children's Chorus provides an authentic vocal model allowing *children to learn from children.* **Project Four: "Using Your Singing Voice"** gives students the opportunity to shape and sustain the five basic singing vowels, understand the relationship of vowel to pitch definition, and apply their skills to the performance of the Renaissance song *Jubilate Deo.* An International Phonetic Alphabet (IPA) Chart for vowels and consonants accompanies the instructional material in Part 2. Much of the Part 2 material is recorded on the *We Will Sing!* cassette.

Part 3 Singing with Musicianship

Part 3 focuses on music reading as an important component of musicianship. Organized contextually around the performance of particular pieces of music, instruction on counting time and reading pitch develops from a related sequence of problem-solving activities derived from the repertoire. The music reading exercises are developed using patterns and excerpts from the performance repertoire. Music reading is introduced by means of music making, then generalized as an introduction to the learning of reading systems. Rhythm syllables and tonic solfa are outlined as a resource for continued skill development to be utilized throughout the entire curriculum. The Practice Projects in Part 3 are not intended as isolated one-time lessons in music reading. The music reading resource is designed to be used regularly throughout the curriculum in every musical context. The development of music reading skill is central to the aims of music performance as music education.

Project Five: "Understanding the Score" orients students to the written page. In the context of Benjamin Britten's arrangement of *The Sally Gardens,* students learn how to follow the score and identify written score markings as an important part of developing overall musicianship. **Project Six: "Feeling Time and Reading Rhythm"** teaches students how to feel pulse, identify meter, conduct, and read rhythm.

Numerous singing, counting, and listening exercises are interwoven throughout the project. **Project Seven: "Hearing Pitch and Reading Notation"** teaches students how to sing solfa, use hand signs to show pitch relationship, identify major and minor tonality, and perform intervals accurately.

Part 4 Singing Together

Part 4 introduces the musical repertoire. Grouped into three distinct Performance Projects, each Program includes six varied compositions, along with detailed musical orientations and optional rehearsal guides. This versatile formatting makes it possible for the classroom teacher or the music specialist to use the materials in a variety of different ways. While the classroom teacher may find the rehearsal guidelines essential in teaching the repertoire, the music specialist may prefer to use the repertoire independently of the rehearsal guide, teaching through an alternative pedagogy. The rehearsal activities in *We Will Sing!* are constructed in such a way that some students may work independently or in small ensemble groups. However they are used, the rehearsal guidelines are developed to encourage a positive musical experience, one that necessarily revolves around classroom singing, develops the student's musicianship, and culminates in musical enjoyment and self-growth.

Performance Projects

Part 4 is comprised of eighteen selected unison and two-part songs appropriate for treble voice students. Grouped into three separate Performance Projects, each group of six songs forms a mini-performance curriculum or concert program of stylistically diverse repertoire suitable for classroom choirs.

Performance Projects: Program One (Fall)

O Music, Sweet Music (Mason)
The Sally Gardens (arr. Britten)
Simple Gifts (arr. Copland)
She's Like the Swallow (arr. Dolloff)
Spring Morning (Henry Carey)
Good Night (Kabalevsky)

Performance Projects: Program Two (Spring)

Jubilate Deo (Praetorius)
The Path to the Moon (Thiman)
I Know Where I'm Goin' (arr. Hughes)
Oliver Cromwell (arr. Britten)
Bist du bei mir (Bach)
Ching-a-Ring Chaw (arr. Copland)

Performance Projects: Program Three (Holiday Celebration)

"Hodie" from A Ceremony of Carols (Britten)
A Child Is Born (Canon)
Poor Little Children (Spiritual)
"How Beautiful are the Feet" from Messiah (Handel)
In Dulci Jubilo (arr. Bach)
Jingle Bell Swing (Elliott)

Orientations

The Orientations provide teachers and students with a detailed musical digest of the repertoire, reflecting the specific elements, form, style, and social-historical background of each work. The teacher-conductor should use the orientation information as an opportunity to encourage the development of musicianship. This feature of the music textbook facilitates teacher planning and enhances the students' knowledge of the musical context.

Rehearsal Guides

The Rehearsal Guide for each song begins with an overview of the musical challenges associated with each work. The Guides develop sequentially beginning with the opportunity to: *(a) produce* the music through singing; *(b) practice* the musicianship necessary to meet the musical challenges; and *(c) perform* the music with skill and understanding. The three-part rehearsal plan invites the satisfaction of a holistic, musical experience.

Produce (Step 1)

In the Production segment of rehearsal, students are engaged in a meaningful form of "musical doing" designed to give them insight into the characteristic features of the particular repertoire. Various methods of introducing the music are recommended depending on the length, character, and complexity of the composition. The initial Production segment of rehearsal should motivate students to develop the skills necessary to perform.

Practice (Step 2)

The Practice segment of rehearsal concentrates on the development of musicianship through musical problem-solving activities designed to teach students how to *think-in-action*. Through participation in rehearsal strategies, students develop the skill and understanding required to perform artistically.

Perform (Step 3)

In the final Performance segment of rehearsal, students apply their musicianship in an *informed production* of the work or section of the work practiced. The student's performance should represent the changes and improvements made during the Practice segment, and serve to synthesize the skills and understandings developed in rehearsal.

Through constant *musical doing* and consistent opportunities for *musical reflecting,* the sequential instruction encourages the development of musicianship and empowers students to succeed. Each lesson-rehearsal finishes with the opportunity to perform the music. The classroom performance must testify to the students' musical understanding. Successful performance is a form of *thinking-in-action* — knowledge that is demonstrated rather than described.[1]

Reflecting and Evaluating

In *We Will Sing!* Practice Projects and Rehearsal Guides, students are assessed throughout the course of instruction. Through graded questions and answers, students are encouraged to describe the musical relationships inherent in the repertoire and challenged to evaluate the performance results of their ensemble. Students regularly reflect on the quality of their work through guided question and answer, peer and teacher evaluation, and written feedback. In each of the Practice Projects, students are invited to complete the problem-solving questions and musical exercises outlined for review at the end of each Project. Similarly, each Rehearsal Guide offers students the opportunity to reflect on and evaluate the results of their performance, by asking them what they liked about their performance and what they would like to improve. After reviewing an audio or video taped performance, students are encouraged to record their reflections in a performance portfolio. Assessment forms offer both quantitative and qualitative evaluation.

Selected Recordings

Each Practice Project and Rehearsal Guide lists selected recordings related to the performance repertoire and the rehearsal experience. To provide a vocal model and performance example, the *We Will Sing!* audio cassette features the Glen Ellyn Children's Chorus singing many of the book's choral titles. Recommended vocal and instrumental recordings related to the performance repertoire feature world class performers in Great Britain, Canada, and United States.

---

1   The CME model of musical instruction is detailed in the author's teaching resource book *Teaching Children Through Choral Music Experience,* Volume 4 (TXB 65). This same model of teaching may be viewed in Segment II of the ACDA video: *On Location with Doreen Rao and the Glen Ellyn Children's Chorus.*

Invitation to Choral Music Experience for Classroom Choirs

for the Teacher-Conductor

Introduction

In his 1988 publication *Music and Education,* Dmitri Kabalevsky says "every class should be a choir." I share the late Russian composer's view, and mourn the many years American music education ignored, even denied choral singing as an integral and foundational aspect of classroom music. But times have changed. Music educators today believe in the innate musical potential of all children and their ability to demonstrate musicality through music making. Recent research supports a praxial view of music education in which the development of musicianship through musical performance is central to self-growth and enjoyment for all children.

Principles of Music Performance as Music Education

Choral Music Experience is a music performance approach to music education. It is a practical, common-sense form of music teaching and learning based on contemporary principles of human development. *We Will Sing!* takes a multicultural view of music education as the opportunity to participate in the concepts, beliefs, and actions of culture. The guiding principles of music performance as music education suggest that: (1) all children have a natural ability to make music; (2) children, like adults, pursue the kinds of experiences that are most enjoyable and self-fulfilling; (3) children's musical perception is codependent upon musical production; (4) music performance as a source of knowledge is a reflection of human experience — it gives the student information about the *self* gained from the student's interaction with the music;

(5) music performance as a form of constructive knowledge develops self-image and self-esteem, perhaps the most important information the child can get.

The Aims of Music Performance

The overall aim of music performance as music education is to achieve self-growth and enjoyment by educating musicianship that will serve the whole person after schooling is over.[2] The two necessary conditions for musical enjoyment are: (1) having something to do (a musical challenge), and (2) developing the ability to do it (know-how). In a choral classroom, the musical challenge is found in the repertoire. The student's ability to meet the musical challenge is determined by the development of musicianship. It is essential to have a balance between the challenges provided by the repertoire and the know-how or musicianship required to perform successfully. Matching the student's musicianship or know-how with an appropriate level of musical challenge propels higher levels of musical learning and more intense musical enjoyment.

A Curriculum for Classroom Choirs

The principles of music performance as music education are demonstrated in *We Will Sing!,* a curriculum for classroom choirs. In a performance approach to music teaching and learning, the repertoire, the development of musicianship, and the opportunity for enjoyment and self-growth form the basis of the curriculum.

---

2   David J. Elliott, *Music Matters: A New Philosophy of Music Education,* Forthcoming.

We Will Sing! is planned as an extended course of study, developed in levels spiraling upward in complexity. This textbook contains seven practice projects and eighteen rehearsal guides. The practice projects and rehearsal guides form a sequence of progressive problem-solving opportunities organized around three separate concert programs. Performance activities derive from authentic musical repertoire and its inherent musical challenges.

In a choral classroom, musicianship is developed from musical problems inherent in the ability to perform particular musical works. In the whole language theory, cognitive and linguistic development are viewed as interdependent. Reading skills are taught from their "real life" use in authentic literature. Patterns and exercises are used in context-specific forms abstracted from the actual literature. Similarly, in music performance as music education, cognitive and musical development are viewed as interdependent. Patterns and exercises used to teach time and pitch are abstracted from particular pieces of music being taught for performance.

In a choral curriculum, teaching and learning develops contextually from the musical opportunities inherent in the study and performance of the repertoire. Children develop musicianship and learn to *think-in-action* by solving real musical problems as they arise in rehearsal and performance. Authentic musical activity of this kind is the only way children gain access to a legitimate musical practice — the kind of musical practice taking place outside the schools — in the real world!

Instructional Methods for Classroom Choirs

In a choral classroom, stylistically diverse and distinctive repertoire forms the centerpiece of instruction. Children develop musicianship from the quality of their music-making for the sake of musical enjoyment and self-growth. Curriculum experts say that music education is situated and contextual. Because every teacher teaches differently and every child learns differently, instructional methods used in *We Will Sing!* offer a guideline rather than a recipe or formula.

In the choral classroom context, the teacher uses both verbal and non-verbal forms of instruction, favoring non-verbal methods as a more musical approach to music teaching. Non-verbal instructional methods include: (1) conducting, (2) use of facial expression, (3) vocal modeling, (4) chanting, (5) solfa, (6) clapping, (7) movement, (8) use of rhythm syllables, (9) playing (piano, guitar, recorder, etc.), and (10) listening. Verbal methods of instruction should be action-centered discussions that encourage students to reflect on their efforts. Verbal methods include: (1) identifying, (2) describing, (3) comparing and contrasting, (4) analyzing, (5) explaining, (6) reviewing, and most importantly (7) evaluating, and (8) judging the results of the students' performance. In a performance context, it is more appropriate (and more musical!) for students to *demonstrate their answers* by singing rather than speaking. The opportunity for students to verbalize their decisions can serve to punctuate, embellish, and reinforce the students' non-verbal understanding.

The Role of the Teacher-Conductor

The principles of music performance as music education suggest that all children have the natural ability and desire to learn. This approach assumes that there are no musically disadvantaged children. In the choral music classroom, the teacher-conductor serves as a guide, coach, facilitator, and mentor who knows: (1) how to advise, coach, and correct the musical problems that arise; (2) how to take time from singing to reflect and think about the quality of the students' performance; (3) how to determine if the students are performing and listening intelligently; and (4) how to motivate and support the students through the musical challenges. The teacher-conductor's expertise also includes: (5) the ability to adjust the instructional goals for learners; (6) direct the students' attention to important musical ideas; and (7) provide knowledge and feedback to the singers as these relate to the form, style, and interpretation of the repertoire.

In the beginning stages of musical development, the teacher-conductor is necessarily more active in supporting and directing the students' progress. During this time, the teacher-conductor may move away from the traditional podium position, vary eye contact, and move among the students. Mouthing words and vocal modeling is a common and often necessary method of instruction at the early stages of musical development. While learning a new work, children require a constant sense of well-being and accomplishment.

As the students develop their musicianship and gain control and self-confidence, they will begin to act autonomously and work together with their teacher-conductor in *musical collaboration.* Musical independence is encouraged and facilitated when the teacher-conductor restricts the more active mode of instruction used at the beginning stages of musical development, in favor of an expressive, controlled, and concise conducting gesture. The conducting gesture itself then becomes a powerful, non-verbal form of musical communication.

The Role of the Student

We Will Sing! invites students to work in a variety of different ways. Some students may be motivated to work independently or in small groups. Where classroom teachers are musically skilled and confident, students will enjoy singing with a large class or group of classes, where they will be motivated by community spirit and group effort. The students can also benefit from the expertise of the artist-teacher whose specialized skill in teaching and conducting will guide and inspire the highest musical standards. In a choral classroom, students remain active and participate in every aspect of music performance, including singing and decision-making.

In music performance, the student is constantly challenged by the opportunity to *produce* music with the singing voice, *practice* the skills and understandings associated with musical challenges in the repertoire, *perform* the improvements, and *evaluate* the results of his/her efforts. Problem-solving, reflecting-on- the-action, and evaluating the musical results encourage the student's continuous participation in decision-making.

When students enjoy the music they are practicing, they are naturally motivated to make musical improvements and develop their musicianship. Given a quality repertoire, nothing is more important for the students than the teacher's musicality, enthusiasm, and expertise.

A Teaching Model for Classroom Choirs

We Will Sing! uses a holistic instructional model that allows young students to work from the concrete musical problems in the repertoire toward the development of musicianship for the sake of musical enjoyment and self-growth. The *produce – practice – perform* model assures that the choir begins with active participation in music making and develops the skills and understandings necessary to meet the musical challenges inherent in the repertoire.

In the *production* segment of the instruction, students are engaged in a meaningful form of "musical doing" which is designed to give them insight into the characteristic features of the particular repertoire. This initial rehearsal segment should motivate the students to develop the skills necessary to *perform.* The *practice* segment of rehearsal concentrates on the development of musicianship required to meet the challenges of the repertoire. Rehearsals are sequenced through musical problem-solving activities designed to teach the students how to *think-in-action,* i.e., how to *demonstrate their knowledge through singing.* In the *performance* segment of rehearsal, students apply their musicianship in an informed production of the work or section of the work practiced. The students' "rehearsal performance" should represent the changes and improvements made during the *practice* segment, and serve to synthesize the skills and understandings developed in rehearsal.

We Will Sing! engages students in the development of their singing voices, a skill central to the music education of every child. The practice projects teach children how to think about their own voices as musical instruments and how to distinguish between singing and speaking. Through performance activities, the children can experiment with different ways of using their voices for ordinary speech and artistic expression. A sequenced series of vocal production exercises includes: (1) warm-up exercises, (2) posture models, (3) breath-management directions, and (4) tone-production vocalizations.

In a choral classroom, instruction must also focus on music reading as an important component of musicianship. Organized contextually around the performance of particular pieces of music, music reading exercises are developed using patterns and excerpts directly from the repertoire or related material. The development of music reading skill is central to the aims of music performance as music education.

Assessment Alternatives for Classroom Choirs

Assessment is an important part of learning in the choral classroom. Based on the Arts Propel Model of Assessment developed at Harvard University, *We Will Sing!* values the development of the student's musicianship and seeks to provide constant feedback to the student. The assessment materials may also supply data for whatever evaluation requirement may be in place in the individual school system. Because the student's perceptual abilities grow naturally out of production experiences, the musical skills

acquired and assessed are closely linked to the actual performance. Critical and reflective thinking skills are formed and assessed in the performance context.

In a choral classroom, teacher-conductors are encouraged to offer continuous feedback and reinforcement to give students a constant sense of well-being and accomplishment.[3] Students should have access to audio and video feedback of their rehearsals and performances on a regular basis.

This book's performance projects and rehearsal guides include several different assessment alternatives. These include: (1) audio and video tapes of solo and group performance. Audio/video feedback is suggested (a) for use by the student for *self-evaluation;* (b) by the group for *peer-evaluation;* and (c) by the teacher for *teacher-evaluation.* Students should have access to audio and video feedback of their rehearsals and performances on a regular basis; (2) Problem-solving exercises integrated into the teaching-learning sequences, reviewed separately at the conclusion of each project. This method of assessment is part of the child's natural engagement in musical activity and does not stop instruction to test for unrelated material; (3) The student's self-directed journal of musical development: *My Performance Portfolio.*

The *We Will Sing!* performance portfolio is a tangible record of the child's musical growth and development — a "biography" of musical challenge and artistic accomplishment developed and maintained over the entire period of instruction. The performance portfolio can include marked scores, audio and/or video tapes, personal reflections, performance critiques, or problem-solving exercise sheets. Simple or elaborate, the performance portfolio should capture the full range of the student's learning and give the student a sense of self-awareness as a developing young artist.

---

3   For a model of this procedure, see the ACDA Video: *On Location with Doreen Rao and the Glen Ellyn Children's Chorus,* available through the American Choral Directors Association. See Appendix, pg. 243.

Invitation to Choral Music Experience for Classroom Choirs

for the Student

Everyone is born with musical ability. We have what is called *innate musical potential.* This simply means we *know* more than we can explain. When we perform music, we are *showing* what we know and how well we know it. If you begin now to develop your own musical potential, you will experience a special form of knowledge, enjoyment, and self-esteem that comes from active participation in musical performance. The following question and answer section will help prepare you for a unique opportunity to develop your musical ability and enjoy musical performance.

How can I develop my musical potential?

First you need the challenges provided by great music. Then you need to master the musical skills required to meet those challenges. Just dabbling in music without skill is not enough. Merely singing through a song will not provide you with valuable information about the music or about yourself. The more skillful your performance, the more you will learn about yourself and the more enjoyment you will find.

The ability to perform music is considered a form of non-verbal knowledge called *musicianship.* As a form of knowledge, musicianship is different from the kind of knowledge required to write tests or verbalize information. Instead of writing or explaining your knowledge, musicianship is *demonstrated* through musical performance. In real life, musicians sing songs, play instruments and compose because they enjoy music, and because they like to show their musicianship through singing, playing, and composing. Musicians find enjoyment when they perform well or when they learn a new work.

What will I learn through music performance?

You will learn authentic musical repertoire, and you will develop the singing skills, rhythm skills, music reading skills, and listening skills necessary to perform artistically. You will learn how to follow a musical score, and you will develop a knowledge of the composer's use of musical elements, form, and style. This knowledge is necessary to interpret music stylistically. This means that you will have the opportunity to develop musicianship and demonstrate your musicianship through singing.

Musicianship is a specialized form of knowledge that requires you to exercise your own judgment in response to the changing sounds of musical works. Performing music involves your ability to listen and to make constant changes and improvements in the quality of your singing. The learning of musicianship takes time, and the ability to master the skills necessary to perform artistically requires concentration and commitment. Doing something well (performing artistically!) is the key to self-growth and enjoyment.

How will I develop my musicianship?

Developing musicianship is not a simple task, but remember, you already have a natural ability in music, and you probably know more about music than you can explain. This music textbook will give you a chance to use what you already know about music, and develop your musicianship through: (1) the vocal production of easy-to-learn musical repertoire; (2) the musical practice and problem-solving opportunities related to the repertoire; and (3) the musical performance and evaluation of your progress.

What are the requirements in music performance?

You will be expected and encouraged to: (1) actively participate in the production of musical works; (2) practice the musical skills necessary to get better and make improvements; and (3) perform and evaluate the results of your efforts. By performing, you are demonstrating your knowledge; by evaluating your performances, you are actively reflecting on the music and the quality of your work. These kinds of problem-solving exercises give you and your teacher the opportunity to assess your *musicianship* and measure your progress.

How can my teacher help me?

Your teacher is an expert who will guide you, coach you, encourage you, and challenge you to develop your singing voice and your musicianship. Your teacher will introduce new songs, lead class discussions, rehearse the repertoire, and conduct the performances. Your teacher will also assess your progress by evaluating your skills and understandings.

How will I be assessed in my music performance program?

In your music performance program you will be assessed on the basis of your individual and class performance of the musical repertoire and the related problem-solving exercises. As an assessment option in this performance program, you can demonstrate your musical development by keeping an individual *performance portfolio.* Your performance portfolio is a record of your musical growth and development. The contents of your performance portfolio will vary according to your teacher's goals, but such an assessment may include any or all of the following options: a journal or diary; problem-solving exercises; performance critiques; and audio/video feedback.

Welcome to *We Will Sing!*

Now that you know what *We Will Sing!* is about and how you can develop your musicianship through musical performance, we invite you to start your exciting musical journey. We wish you the knowledge, enjoyment, and self-esteem that comes from active participation in musical performance.

M Y   P E R F O R M A N C E   P O R T F O L I O

A Record of Musical Growth

Name:_____ Date:_____

Your performance portfolio may include:

A *journal or diary* made up of class notes, cassette recordings, personal reflections, marked scores, and your teacher's feedback.

The *Problem-Solving Exercises* found at the conclusion of each practice project in Parts 2 and 3.

Performance critiques in which *you* have the opportunity to judge the results of your ensemble's performance by *identifying* the musical problem you hear, *prescribing* at least one possible solution, and *reviewing* the outcomes.

A *cassette tape recording* or *video recording* of your work in practice projects and performance project programs.

PART 2

Singing

Part 2
Singing

Part 2 Practice Projects concentrate on vocal development and stress the use of the singing voice as a musical instrument. The vocal lessons teach students to distinguish between the speaking voice and the singing voice. Through a series of problem-solving exercises, students are encouraged to experiment with different ways of using their voices for ordinary speech and artistic expression. Singing posture, breath manage- ment, and tone production exercises are directed through the use of textbook directions, photographic illustrations and diagrams, and cassette tape instructions. The Glen Ellyn Children's Chorus recordings provide an authentic vocal model for classroom choirs. Each practice project offers students the opportunity to apply their vocal skills in the performance of familiar repertoire.

Practice Project One
Your Singing Voice

In Practice Project One, you will sing the song, *O Music, Sweet Music* for the first time. You will have the opportunity to learn: (1) how to use your voice as a musical instrument; and (2) how to distinguish between singing some-thing and saying something. Follow the directions for each section and review this material regularly.

Sing Lowell Mason's famous school song.

Ex. 1. O Music, Sweet Music
We Will Sing! cassette, side 1

Describe Your First Performance

Can you describe how you sounded when you sang Lowell Mason's song *O Music, Sweet Music* for the first time? Did you sing the right notes at the right time? Was your first performance ac-curate and expressive? **Describe** any changes and improvements you would like to make.

If you have decided that you would like to improve your performance and get better at what you are doing, you must first learn how to use your voice as a *musical instrument*. When you achieve that goal, you will feel and hear the difference in your performance. We invite you to listen carefully to your teacher's instructions and practice the material that follows.

Using Your Voice as a Musical Instrument

Singing Lowell Mason's song *O Music, Sweet Music* requires that you use your voice as a musical instrument. Using your voice to *sing* something may be different from the way you use your voice to *say* something. Singing re-quires *concentration, coordination* and *control*. When you learn to use your voice as a musical instrument, you will be able to make the changes necessary to perform well and enjoy singing for its own sake.

Singing is an enjoyable and musical way of using your voice. Everyone has a singing voice, although many people have never learned to sing. Some historians believe that humans sang before learning to speak and that speech prob-ably developed from singing. In certain cultures everybody sings from infancy to old age. There are even countries where people sing *more* than they speak.

In our country, there are many different ways people use their singing voices. Some people use their singing voices to sing jazz or opera as a solo artist. Some people use their singing voices to sing pop or classical music in ensembles, or to sing in the traditional style of their cultural heritage.

Listening to Vocal Artists

You may enjoy listening to examples of celebrated solo performers like jazz artist Ella Fitzgerald or opera artist Kiri Te Kanawa (see the *Selected Recordings* list). Examples of ensemble singing include the celebrated Atlanta Symphony Chorus, the innovative Gregg Smith Singers, and the well known Manhattan Transfer. Examples of ritual or traditional singing include Navajo chant, Inuit throat singing, and Black gospel. **Compare** and **contrast** how different singers and choirs use their voices to perform.

Even without instruction, some students can sing clearly and tunefully because of their family traditions or musical opportunities. Most people learn to use their singing voices in schools where they are taught by music teachers who have special knowledge about the singing voice. **Listen** to a recording of the Glen Ellyn Children's Chorus singing Dmitri Kabalevsky's *Good Night* (*We Will Sing!* cassette, side 2). These students have learned to sing with musicianship. They know how to use their singing voices with skill and understanding.

You and Your Singing Voice

You can do many things with your singing voice. You can explore the pitch, time, and text ideas of music. You can experience different styles of music from traditional folk songs such as the Newfoundland ballad *She's Like the Swallow* to contemporary composed music like Benjamin Britten's "Hodie" from *A Ceremony of Carols.*

You can sing in a choir, or you can sing alone as a soloist. It's fun to sing a solo. It is also fun to sing in a choir. Singing in a choir gives you the opportunity to work together with others to create something that can change your life.

Your singing voice is unique, but it can also be compared to other kinds of musical instruments. To perform on the flute, the piano, or the violin takes regular practice. Just as performing on these musical instruments requires practice, performing with your singing voice also requires regular practice. And, like playing an instrument in an orchestra, singing in a choir brings great personal pleasure.

Summary

Knowing how to perform with your singing voice is a specialized form of knowledge that will help you understand the musics of many styles and many cultures. Music performance is a way of knowing more about yourself and knowing more about others. Singing in a choir can be a way of enjoying music throughout your lifetime.

Selected Recordings

You may enjoy listening to these performances by selected vocal artists.

Ella Fitzgerald:

Ella and Louis Again. Ella Fitzgerald, vocals; Louis Armstrong vocals, trumpet. Verve CD 825 374-2.

Kiri Te Kanawa:

Ave Maria. Kiri Te Kanawa, soprano; Choir of St. Paul's Cathedral, Barry Rose, conductor. Philips 412 629-2 (also 629-4; LD 629-1).

The Atlanta Symphony Chorus, Robert Shaw, director:

Symphony of Psalms. The Atlanta Symphony Orchestra and Chorus, Robert Shaw, conductor. Telarc CD-80254.

The Gregg Smith Singers:

America Sings: American Choral Music after 1950. The Gregg Smith Singers, Gregg Smith, conductor. Turnabout TV 34759.

Manhattan Transfer:

The Offbeat of Avenues. The Manhattan Transfer. Atlantic 7-81233-2.

Navajo Chant:

Navajo Songs from Canyon de Chelly. New World Records 80406-2.

Songs of the Earth, Winter, Fire and Sky: Music of the American Indians. New World Records 80246-2.

Inuit Throat Singing:

Inuit Throat and Harp Songs: Eskimo Women's Music of Povungnituk. Canadian Music Heritage Collection MH001.

Black Gospel:

Jubilation III: Glory Train. The Montreal Jubilation Gospel Choir, Trevor Payne, director. Justin Time Record, Inc. JUST 35-2.

M Y   P E R F O R M A N C E   P O R T F O L I O

Problem-Solving Exercises

Name:_____ Date:_____

1. **Describe** your first performance of Lowell Mason's song *O Music, Sweet Music.*

2. **Decide** what you liked about your performance and what you would like to improve for the next time.

3. What are the benefits of learning to use your voice as a musical instrument?

4. **Describe** some of the different ways people use their singing voice.

5. How did the Glen Ellyn Children's Chorus use their singing voices in the recorded performance of **Good Night** (*We Will Sing!* cassette, side 1)?

6. What are some of the benefits of singing in a choir?

Practice Project Two
Finding Your Singing Voice

In Practice Project Two you will have the opportunity to: (1) perform the song, *O Music, Sweet Music* with your singing voice; (2) compare and contrast the singing voice with the speaking voice; and (3) experiment with different ways of using your voice for ordinary speech and artistic expression. Follow the directions for each section and review this material regularly.

Sing *O Music, Sweet Music.*

Ex. 1. O Music, Sweet Music
We Will Sing! cassette, side 1

Ways of Using Your Voice

People use their voices in many different ways. Singing is a special way of using your voice. It is different from speaking, laughing, crying, cheering, or sighing. When you use your voice for speaking, you use breath and you use words with personal meaning. When you use your voice for singing, you also use breath and words, but you use them with a musical "goal-in-mind."

The Stage Voice

Actors who work in the theater use the speaking voice in two highly differentiated ways. In everyday conversation, the actor's voice can sound ordinary, just like anyone else's voice. But on stage, the actor's voice may sound darker, louder, and stronger. The actor's stage voice is a way of using the speaking voice for dramatic purposes. Try this experiment:

Speak these words in your actor's "stage voice" as if it were necessary to communicate in a large theater to a large audience.

O music, sweet music,
thy praises we will sing.

Your Speaking Voice

Your *speaking voice* is most commonly used as an "everyday" way of communicating thoughts and feelings. But like the actor's stage voice which is used for dramatic purposes only, the *singing voice* is a musical way of creating the ideas of a song and carrying them to an audience. When speaking, you must breathe and form words that represent your thoughts. In singing, breath and words form musical ideas.

When you use your ordinary speaking voice, you are not always aware that you are breathing. Likewise, you may not be consciously aware of how the words sound. The action and your awareness of the action are not connected. But when you use your singing voice, you are consciously aware of your breathing (especially at the beginning stages) and you will use both breath and words with a musical "goal-in-mind." Do you know why? Consider these important ideas.

Comparing Speaking and Singing

When you sing a word, the length of the sound is *longer* than when you speak the same word. When you compare speaking a sentence with singing a phrase, you will soon discover that your singing voice requires *more* breath in order to lengthen and sustain the sound. Try this exercise.

Speak these words in your *everyday speaking voice:*

> *O music, sweet music,*
> *thy praises we will sing.*
> *We will tell of the pleasures*
> *and happiness you bring.*
> *Music, music, let the chorus sing.*

Sing the same words in your *musical singing voice* as you learned to use it in Practice Project One.

The quality of your musical *singing voice* is louder and stronger than the quality of your everyday *speaking voice.* For this reason, your singing voice requires more breath, more energy and more control than your speaking voice.

Using Your Own Voice

There are many different ways you can use your own voice. Speaking, sighing, crying, groaning, yawning, and whispering are just some different ways of using the voice. You can probably think of other ways to use your voice, common ways and unusual ways. You may enjoy producing a variety of vocal sounds.

Speak these same words in your *quiet whisper voice.* Experiment with various speaking voices changing the speed, volume, and tone.

> *O music, sweet music,*
> *thy praises we will sing...*

Speak the same words in the *voice of your choice.*

> *O music, sweet music,*
> *thy praises we will sing...*

Singing may seem very close to speaking, but singing is a special way of using the voice. Some teachers say that singing is an extension of speech. For many people, singing may be a *new* way of using the voice. As you probably discovered earlier, the musical singing voice requires more breath support, more energy, and more control than the everyday speaking voice. Let's try to find *your* singing voice.

Speech Patterns

Here are some activities that may help you discover the difference between your ordinary speaking voice and your musical singing voice. **Vocalize** these everyday speech patterns shown in Ex. 2. **Listen** for the varying pitch levels or what we call *intonation,* the "up and down" of the speaking voice.

Ex. 2. Everyday Speech Patterns

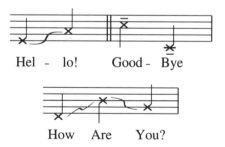

Follow these instructions: (1) **Listen** to the class chant the speech patterns shown in Ex. 2. (2) **Listen** to individual voices as they speak the same patterns. (3) **Listen** for the variation between voice qualities. (4) **Listen** for light sounding voices, heavy sounding voices, bright voices, dark voices, loud voices, soft voices, small voices, and big voices. (5) **Vocalize** these familiar, "everyday" ways of using your voice shown in Ex. 3:

Ex. 3. Everyday Use of Your Voice

Yawn: Sigh:

Laugh/Cry:

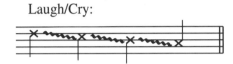

Vocal Range

Remember, the "everyday" speaking voice is used for personal expression, and the singing voice is used for musical expression. It is important to expand the *range* (the high and low) of your speaking voice as it begins to extend to your singing voice. When you find your singing voice, you will become aware of the significant difference in the range between these two types of voices. The range of your speaking voice is probably less than one octave as shown in Ex. 4.

Ex. 4. Speaking Voice Range (pitch not exact):

In contrast, the *range* of your singing voice can easily approach two octaves as shown in Ex. 5.

Ex. 5. Singing Voice Range (for treble voice):

Summary

As you have learned, people use their voices in many different ways. Humans have been singing since the beginning of time. Singing is a way of expressing feelings, ideas, and important information. Unlike anything else, the human voice is closely associated with personal feeling. Learning to use your singing voice is a way you can learn more about yourself and others. The better you sing, the more you will learn. Knowing how to use your singing voice will come from practicing and performing regularly. Your participation in these songs and exercises will help you achieve these important goals.

Practice Project Two

M Y   P E R F O R M A N C E   P O R T F O L I O

Problem-Solving Exercises

Name:_____ Date:_____

1. **Compare** the differences between your speaking voice and your singing voice.

2. How is the singing voice different from the speaking voice?

3. How is breath use in singing different from breath use in speaking?

4. **Compare** and **contrast** the vocal range of the speaking voice with the vocal range of the singing voice.

5. **List** three different ways you can use your own voice.

6. **Listen** to the recording of Lowell Mason's *O Music, Sweet Music* on *We Will Sing!* cassette, side 1. Determine what kind of voice the choir is using and describe the quality of the voices you hear.

Practice Project Three
Exercising Your Singing Voice

In Practice Project Three, you will have the opportunity to develop the vocal skills necessary to perform and enjoy singing. Specifically, you will learn: (1) how to position your body as a musical instrument; (2) how to manage your breath for singing; and (3) how to exercise your singing voice to produce musical tone. Follow the directions for each section and review this material regularly.

Remembering *Practice Project Two,* review the important differences between the *everyday speaking voice* and the *musical singing voice.* Through the following songs and exercises, you will learn how to make the changes necessary to perform musically and enjoy the experience of singing.

Knowing how to produce your singing voice will come from practicing exercises and vocalizations while you are learning new songs. Practicing your singing voice requires a short preparation time called a *warm-up.* During the warm-up time you may sing these exercises alone or with your class.

There are four important steps in preparing your voice for singing. Each step is basic to developing healthy singing habits. These exercises should be carefully practiced in the suggested order. The pictures will show you how to follow the instructions.

1. Exercise

Exercising your body prepares you for singing, just as athletic exercises prepare an athlete for the game. Exercising requires *concentration, coordination,* and *control;* exercise conditions the muscles and the mind for singing. Complete this short series of exercises.

1(a). Five long stretches up

1(b). Five long stretches down

(a) Five long stretches up.
Raise your hands high over the head as if reaching for the sky. Pull the entire body upward, pushing up from the toes to the finger tips.

(b) Five long stretches down.
Bending over, touch your toes. Your head should hang down, and your arms should be loose. The head, neck, and arms should feel loose and heavy. On a count of five, gradually unwind from the lower back, keeping the head released down and the arms loose.

(c) Rotate the shoulders forward in circular motion five times.
Move them all the way around, slowly.

(d) Gently drop the head forward and rotate very slowly from side to side.

1(d). Head rotation

1(e). Face massage

(e) Gently massage the face and jaw with the back of the hands. Do this slowly.
This exercise will rid you of possible tension in the jaw and tongue.

(f) Rotate the shoulders backward in circular motion five times.
Rotate all the way around, slowly. On the fifth rotation, gently drop the shoulders back and down. This exercise positions the upper body into a singing posture.

2. Posture

Good singing posture is basic to knowing how to sing. Your body itself is your singing voice. The physical position of your body affects the way you breathe and the way you sound. Your ability to produce singing tone depends on the physical position of the body. *The way you look influences the way you sound.* It is better to stand when singing. If you are sitting, sit in a standing position at the front edge of the chair with your back straight. Follow these simple steps:

2(a). Singing posture

(a) Keep your feet slightly apart.
Keep your body facing forward and your weight evenly distributed. Knees may be slightly bent. Avoid a tight or "locked" position in the knees.

(b) Keep your hands at your side.
Do not fold your hands in front or back. It is important to avoid any body tension. Keep a mental image of "heavy hands" hanging at your side.

(c) Keep your upper body placed high.
Your chest should be high, shoulders rotated back and hanging down. Avoid raising your shoulders up, as this will interrupt the air flow and close off the open space necessary for singing.

2(d). Natural alignment

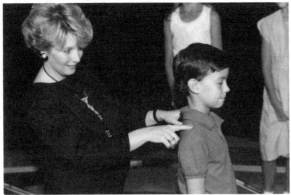

(d) Keep your head evenly and naturally aligned with the spinal column.
Be aware of your head position. Avoid stretching or "reaching" for the high notes as this is unhealthy and can lead to vocal problems.

(e) Remember:
Good singing posture is the key to proper breath management and healthy tone production.

3. Breathing

Breathing and Tone Production segments of Practice Project Three can be heard on the We Will Sing! cassette, side 1

Breathing is the most important part of healthy, in-tune singing. Without proper breath management, you cannot use your singing voice. When you breathe properly, all the important spaces in the throat open for singing. The result is a rich and resonant tone quality. The ability to manage the breath for singing depends on practice. The following exercises will help you develop this important skill.

(a) The "cold air sip."
Form your lips for an (oo) vowel, as if sipping through a straw. Draw the air in slowly through the (oo) formation. Inhale slowly over the count of three. Exhale slowly over the count of five on a *ts* (hissing) sound. Gradually extend the exhalation period from five to ten to fifteen counts.

Ex. 1. The "cold air sip"

(oo) ——————— 'ts' ——————— *(repeat)*
inhale   *exhale*

Remember that during exhalation, posture is very important! Keep your shoulders back and your upper body placed high. Control your body posture and do not collapse forward during exhalation.

3(a). The cold air sip (inhale)

The cold air sip (exhale)

(b) Short rhythmic staccato breathing.
Practice these repeated patterns several times. This exercise will gradually strengthen the muscles used in breathing. Repeat this exercise at different rates of fast and slow and with varying levels of loud and soft.

Ex. 2. Staccato breathing

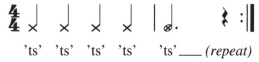

'ts' 'ts' 'ts' 'ts'   'ts'___ *(repeat)*

3(b). Staccato breathing

(c) "Cleansing air breath."
Through your nose, inhale all the way using full lung capacity. Slowly release the breath through loosely closed lips.

Optional Breathing Exercises:

(d) Pant like a dog.

(e) Blow out the candle in short, staccato spurts.

(f) Piff, puff, poof.
With emphasis on the consonant "p" make a short, rhythmic chant on this sequence of sounds.

(g) Blowing bubbles in a milkshake.
Using very loose lips, mimic the sound of bubble blowing from low to high pitch and back to low.

• Adapt these exercises to reflect the rhythmic motives of the repertoire being studied.

4. Tone Production

Breathing and Tone Production segments of Practice Project Three can be heard on the We Will Sing! cassette, side 1.

Sung sounds are longer and stronger than spoken sounds. While singing tone begins with breath, the vowel lengthens pitch and colors tone. Singing tone is directly related to vowel color. Tone can be bright, like the (ee) sound in the word "me," or it can be dark, like the (oo) sound in the word "too." Choosing vowel colors for singing is like choosing water colors for painting. There are many different kinds of tone. Each piece of music requires a variety of different colors depending on text, language, and style of the music.

Your ability to produce the singing voice depends on your ability to color tone. Vowel color determines pitch. To control pitch, you must sustain the vowel on the breath, and you must change the vowel color when it is necessary to improve the pitch. The following exercises will help you learn how to sing vowels correctly and improve pitch.

As you practice your singing voice, you will develop musical control. Singing with skill will give you the confidence you need to enjoy performing many different styles of music. Complete the following exercises:

(a) Speak the five basic singing vowels:
Begin by speaking slowly, sustaining the pure vowel without interruption by the diphthong. (A *diphthong* is a complex vowel sound that occurs in a word like "ride," in which the (ah) vowel continues into an (ee) vowel on the same syllable.) Vowel formation is essential for good singing. The shape of the vowel, supported by the breath, directs vocal tone.

Speak the following exercise:

IPA Symbol	Phonetic Sound	Word Example
[i]	(ee)	m<u>e</u>
[e]	(ay)	<u>a</u>te
[ɑ]	(ah)	f<u>a</u>ther
[o]	(oh)	<u>o</u>bey
[u]	(oo)	t<u>oo</u>

Speak the next exercise which combines these vowels:

"Me, I ate the cake for my father to obey.
I ate too much."

(b) The "sip and sigh."
Inhale through the "cold air sip" (exercise 3(a)) over the count of three. Release the air slowly and easily on an open (ah) vowel, descending in a slide from high to low. Maintain the same vowel sound throughout the descending line. Check your posture to insure that your chest and shoulders do not collapse forward as the pitch descends. Place your index finger gently on your lower jaw while you sustain the (ah) vowel through the descending line (glissando). The tone quality should remain supported and evenly colored throughout the vocal range.

Ex. 3. Glissando on the (ah) vowel

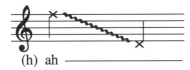

(h) ah ————

4(b). "Sighing" on the ah vowel

Repeat the **"sip and sigh"** exercise on a vocal glissando from low to high to low on the (oo) vowel.

Ex. 4. Glissando on the (oo) vowel

(h) (oo) ————————————

4(b). "Sighing" on the (oo) vowel

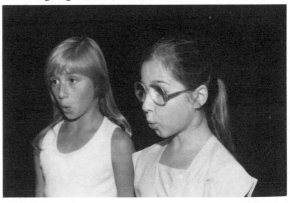

(c) Unison nee [i], nay [e], nah [ɑ], no [o], nu [u].
Practice the five basic singing vowels preceded by the consonant "n." This voiced consonant places the vowel in a "forward" position, making it easier for you to feel and hear the pitch. Sing these vowel progressions in unison, moving up by half steps. Sustain the pure vowel on each pitch.

Ex. 5. Singing the five basic vowels

ni ne na no nu ——

ni ne na no nu ——

ni ne *etc.*

ni ne *(repeat syllables)*

(d) Descending (oo).

Singing on a descending (oo) vowel will exercise your head voice (the singing voice). This exercise will bring the open (oo) space into the middle and lower ranges of your voice. As you inhale, you should have a sense of open space in your mouth and throat, as if there is an orange or grapefruit inside. Repeat this progression several times listening for good intonation and evenness of tone color throughout the range.

Ex. 6. Descending (oo) vowel

(h) (oo) _____

(oo) _____

(e) Ascending octave, slow, descending arpeggios.

Singing this exercise will help you sustain the basic vowels within a wide singing range. For comfort and evenness of tone, try this exercise with the back of your hands placed gently on the face so the jaw drops and the tongue falls forward.

Ex. 7. Descending arpeggios

Nah _____

Nah _____

(f) "Noah's Ark."

Practice this vowel combination throughout the range of your singing voice. Sing this vocal exercise moving up by half steps. Sing only as high as your voice feels comfortable.

Ex. 8. "Noah's Ark"

No-ah, No-ah, No-ah, No-ah, No-ah, No-ah, No-ah's Ark!
repeat

Summary

As you practice the vocal exercises in *Practice Project Three,* you will soon *feel* a difference in the way you are able to produce and control your singing voice You will also *hear* the difference in the way your voice sounds when you sing the performance repertoire.

Selected Recordings

We Will Sing! cassette, side 1. "Breathing and Tone Exercises" by members of the Glen Ellyn Children's Chorus.

M Y   P E R F O R M A N C E   P O R T F O L I O

Problem-Solving Exercises

Name:_____ Date:_____

1. **Describe** the four steps which prepare your voice for singing.

2. **Describe** how good posture affects your singing voice.

3. **Listen** to the *We Will Sing!* cassette, side 1 and **practice** the breath exercises with the tape. How does breath management affect your singing voice?

4. **Listen** to the *We Will Sing!* cassette, side 1 and **practice** the tone production exercises with the tape. **Describe** how vocal color affects tone.

5. **Record** your own voice on cassette tape or **listen** to your choir warm-up tapes and **describe** any improvements you hear in the quality of the singing tone.

6. In your performance portfolio journal, keep a record of your practice and the continuing changes you hear in your choir's tone quality.

Practice Project Four
Using Your Singing Voice

In Practice Project Four, you will have the opportunity to: (1) exercise the skills necessary to shape and sustain the five basic singing vowels: ee [i], ay [e], ah [ɑ], o [o], oo [u]; (2) understand the relationship of vowel color to pitch accuracy; and (3) apply your skills to the Renaissance song *Jubilate Deo*. A learning resource for vowels and consonants appears at the end of this project. Follow the directions for each section and review this material regularly.

Your ability to use your singing voice as a musical instrument is related to your ability to shape and sustain the pure vowel. When the vowel is supported on the breath and shaped by the mouth, your vocal tone will be rich and resonant.

Experiment with vowel color starting with the bright (ee) [i] vowel and then the darker (oo) [u] vowel. Deciding on a vowel color is like choosing a color for painting. The color red for example, results in a particular visual effect. Similarly, the (ah) [ɑ] vowel results in a particular tonal effect.

When a vowel color is too dark, the tone produced may be heard flat or out of tune. When the vowel color is too bright, the tone produced may be heard sharp or out of tune. Changing or modifying the vowel color can improve the pitch. Follow these exercises in preparation for your next performance.

Shaping the Vowel

Shaping the vowel creates color and defines pitch. Shaping the vowel improves intonation.

(a) **Speak the five singing vowels slowly.**
Listen for the long, sustained quality of the pure vowel sound:

(ee)	(ay)	(ah)	(oh)	(oo)
[i]	**[e]**	**[ɑ]**	**[o]**	**[u]**

(b) **Vocalize the same vowels on the voiced consonant [n].**
Vocalizing the consonant [n] will help you place the vowel "forward" in the mouth. The [n] will add resonance to the tone.

Ex. 1.

ni ne na no nu ——

ni ne na no nu ——

ni ne *etc.*

ni ne *(repeat syllables)*

(c) After your class sings the exercise in Ex. 1, **listen** to one another in small groups or individually. **Sing** these vowels and work to achieve a full and resonant vocal tone. Avoid making a thin or strident sound. When you shape and support the vowel on the breath, and when the tone is resonant, you may begin to feel a ringing sensation, or what can be understood as the movement of vibrations inside the vocal tract. The "ring" you feel is a form of sense impression produced by vibrations felt from the movement of the tone. It is called a *kinesthetic sense impression*. Singers hear the tone by feeling the tone.

(d) After you sing the exercise shown in Ex. 1, **describe:** (1) the way the tone *feels;* and (2) the way the tone *sounds.* If the sound you are producing is still thin or strident, place index fingers gently into the corners of the lips so that your lips are rounded into an (oo) [u] shape. This exercise will create more open space inside the vocal tract, and you will **feel** and **hear** the tone as much more resonant.

(d) Shaping the (oo) [u] vowel

(e) After you have practiced the five singing vowels and your vocal tone is rich and resonant, the entire class should **vocalize** together. **Listen** to the important change in tone quality. **Describe** the tone you *now* hear.

(f) **Sing** *Jubilate Deo,* shown in Ex. 2. In your performance of this song, sustain the pure vowel sounds. This will help you sing in tune.

Ex. 2. Jubilate Deo

In your vocal performance of *Jubilate Deo* there should be an evenness of tone quality throughout the song so that both the (ay) [e] vowels sound the same: *Jubilate Deo.* (A discussion on consonants in choral singing appears at the end of Practice Project Four.)

(g) After you sing *Jubilate Deo,* **describe** the sensations you experienced. Did you have trouble singing the highest note? If so, perhaps you will need to *modify* the vowel to sound more open. Place the index finger on your jaw as you breathe to sing the (ah) [ɑ] vowel. This exercise will help you lower the jaw, shape the vowel, and improve the intonation. (A short discussion on vowel modification appears on the next page.)

Vocal Diction

Vocal diction is an important part of good singing. Your ability to sing musically depends on the way you use vowels and consonants to shape and define the tone. The following vowel and consonant chart will guide singers in making diction choices. Use this material as a reference.

International Phonetic Alphabet

The International Phonetic Alphabet (IPA) is an important tool in choral singing. The IPA can by used by students to analyze both vowels and consonants. It is a phonetic symbol system useful in every language, and it is a common way of making pronunciation decisions in all forms of vocal music. Choral music is defined by text made up of vowels and consonants. Using text in a thoughtful manner is the key to performing choral music expressively. The following chart is an abbreviated guide for the teacher and the student.

Vowels

Vowels in choral music create color and define pitch. The sung vowel also carries and sustains tone. In making decisions about vowel color, consult this vowel chart, then speak the words to the song slowly and rhythmically. This vowel chanting exercise will transfer accurately to the singing voice.

The Five "Basic" Singing Vowels

IPA Symbol	English Word
[i]	key, see
[e]	ch<u>ao</u>s, beige
[ɑ]	father, calm
[o]	obey, note
[u]	too, moon

Other Common Vowels in Singing

[ae]	hat, and
[ɔ]	tall, call
[ɛ]	wed, met
[ɪ]	it, busy
[ʊ]	pull, wolf

Neutral Vowels

[ʌ]	up, of (stressed)
[ə]	alone (unstressed)

Diphthongs

[ɑɪ]	night, white
[eɪ]	day, gray
[ou]	no, rose
[ɑu]	now, brow
[ju]	you, piu

Vowel Modification

Vowel modification can be described as a way of producing a desired tone color (timbre). When singing up or down a scale, singers often adjust the vowel color to preserve the beauty of the tone. Vowel modification is also used to assure good intonation and good diction. The ability to modify vowels requires the singer to choose a brighter or darker sound for a particular vowel. Singing together requires that all members of the choir agree on a particular vowel color or vowel modification.

Vowel Chart Using IPA Symbols

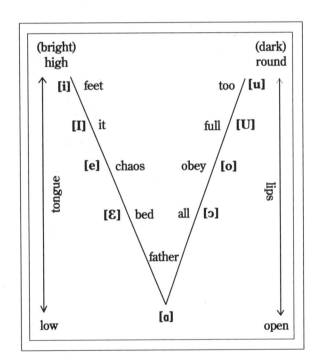

a Phonetic Cat

Consonants

Consonants in choral music create articulation and define rhythm. The consonant starts and stops pitch. The consonant also acts to join pitches and separate pitches. Some consonants can add color or resonance to the tone quality. For example, the consonant [L] tends to pull the tone back in the throat and darken the vowel, while the consonant [n] places the tone "forward" in the mouth and brightens the vowel. Consonants which focus the vowel forward and produce resonance are often preferable for developing young voices.

Voiced Consonants	**Unvoiced Consonants**
(requires phonation)	(requires air but not phonation)
[d] <u>d</u>ead	[t] <u>t</u>ent
[v] <u>v</u>isit	[f] <u>f</u>ather
[b] <u>b</u>ow	[p] <u>p</u>epper
[g] <u>g</u>ive, <u>g</u>o	[k] <u>q</u>uick
[ð] <u>th</u>e	[θ] (th) <u>th</u>in
[z] ro<u>s</u>e	[s] <u>s</u>imple
[ʒ] fu<u>s</u>ion, A<u>s</u>ia	[ʃ] (sh) <u>sh</u>ine
[d₃] <u>j</u>ustice	[tʃ] (ch) <u>ch</u>eer
[L] <u>l</u>aw	(no partner)
[j] <u>y</u>ou	(no partner)
[w] <u>w</u>ell	[hw] (wh) <u>wh</u>ere
(no partner)	[h] <u>h</u>ouse

Using Phonetic Analysis

Identify the vowels and consonants you will sing in the Latin motet *Jubilate Deo.* Using the IPA Symbols, analyze each syllable:

Ju -	**bi -**	**la -**	**te**	**De -**	**o.**
[ju]	[bi]	[Lɑ]	[te]	[de]	[o]

Al -	**le -**	**lu -**	**ia!**
[ɑ]	[Lɛ]	[Lu]	[ja]

Rules for Singing r

There are three general rules regarding the vocalization of [r]:

1. **Neutralized [r]**
   Negate the [r] or change it to a neutral vowel [ə]. Negate [r] when it is precedes a consonant, or when it is at the end of a word (hea̶rt,   me̶rcy,   cha̶rm,   Lo̶rd, eve̶r).

2. **Sung [r]**
   Sing the [r] in popular or folk style; always lengthen the vowel sound before the [r] and then get rid of it as quickly as possible. The [r] is sung (not negated!) when it appears before a vowel (a<u>r</u>ise, dea<u>r</u>est).

3. **Flipped [r]**
   Flip or roll the [r] in opera, sacred choral music, and when there are many voices singing together. The ability to flip or roll the [r] depends on the vocal range. It is easier to flip the [r] on a high pitch.

Summary

In choral singing, vocal diction is the key to success. The vowel creates color and defines pitch. The consonant creates articulation and defines rhythm.

For more information on the musical function of text in choral music, see Choral Music Experience Volume 3, *The Art in Choral Music,* p. 10 (TXB 64).

Selected Recordings

We Will Sing! cassette, side 1. "Breathing and Tone Production Exercises" by members of the Glen Ellyn Children's Chorus.

M Y   P E R F O R M A N C E   P O R T F O L I O

Problem-Solving Exercises

Name:_____ Date:_____

1. How does shaping the vowel improve pitch?

2. **Describe** what you feel when you shape and support the vowel on the breath.

3a. **Sing** *Julbiate Deo* and **identify** five pure vowel sounds.

Ju – bi – la – te De – o.   Ju – bi – la – te

De – o.   Al – le – lu – ia!

3b. From the International Phoenetic Alphabet Chart, **choose** the IPA Symbols that you think represent the desired vowel colors. **Mark** your choice under each separate vowel in the example above.

4. **Describe** how to modify the (ah) [a] vowel in "Jubi<u>la</u>te."

5. What are the functions of vowels and consonants in choral music?

PART 3

Singing With Musicianship

Part 3
Singing with Musicianship

Part 3 Practice Projects focus on the development of music reading skills as an important component of musicianship. Instruction on counting time and reading pitch is organized sequentially through a series of problem-solving exercises developed from the challenges of the repertoire.

Practice Project Five
Understanding the Score

In Practice Project Five, you will have the opportunity to: (1) examine the function of the written score as it applies to developing musicianship; (2) develop the tools to aid in the interpretation of music notation; and (3) identify ways the written score markings influence how a musician makes decisions about performing a musical work. Follow the directions for each section and review this material regularly.

The written score is the visual representation of a composer's intentions. Indeed, the written score, also called *musical notation,* is only a rough approximation of the composer's intent and should not be confused with the music itself. Musicians are called upon to not only learn the language of the visual roadmap, the written score, but to then make many musical decisions about how the piece is to be produced, practiced, and ultimately, performed.

These musical decisions are at the core of developing musicianship. Interpreting the written score is an important facet of musical understanding. Developing the skills necessary to understand the musical notation forms a strong foundation for developing overall musicianship and should be regarded as a continuing journey of discovery.

Musicians frequently "see" something new in the written score after many months or years of studying the same work. Like all aspects of music learning, examining and interpreting written notation is a process, not an end.

How, then, does the process of following a score begin? The young musician must develop a set of tools to help in this discovery, the first of which is orientation to the music page.

Following the Score

Benjamin Britten's arrangement, *The Sally Gardens,* will serve as a working example as you begin to examine musical notation. Each specific term is numbered in the text below, and in the corresponding area in the music. Use this section for class discussion or for independent learning.

Music reading, like reading the English language, takes place from left to right. Many young students have a strong connection to words and can initially follow a score by following the printed text.

1. Text
In the example provided, find the first word of the *text* in *The Sally Gardens.* Using a finger as a guide, speak the text aloud. Note that the text does not begin right away, but enters in the middle of the page. Why would this be, and what instrument is sounding before the entrance of the voices?

2. Vocal Line
By examining the top left portion of the page, one discovers that the *vocal line,* labeled "voices," is notated above the *instrumental line,* labeled "piano." Observe also that while the words are spoken as sentences, some words are hyphenated. These markings merely match syllables of words to specific notes placed directly above.

3. Treble Clef
The vocal line is notated in the *treble clef* (𝄞). The treble clef represents pitches commonly associated with the female, or unchanged male voices. Notice the instrumental line uses the treble clef in the piano part.

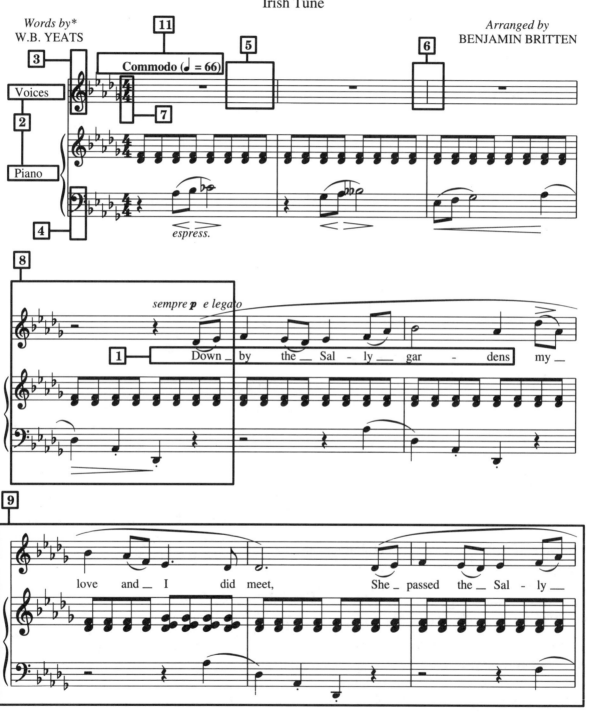

To Clytie Mundy

THE SALLY GARDENS
Irish Tune

Words by*
W.B. YEATS

Arranged by
BENJAMIN BRITTEN

*The words of this song are reprinted from "Collected Poems of W.B. Yeats" by permission of Mrs. Yeats.

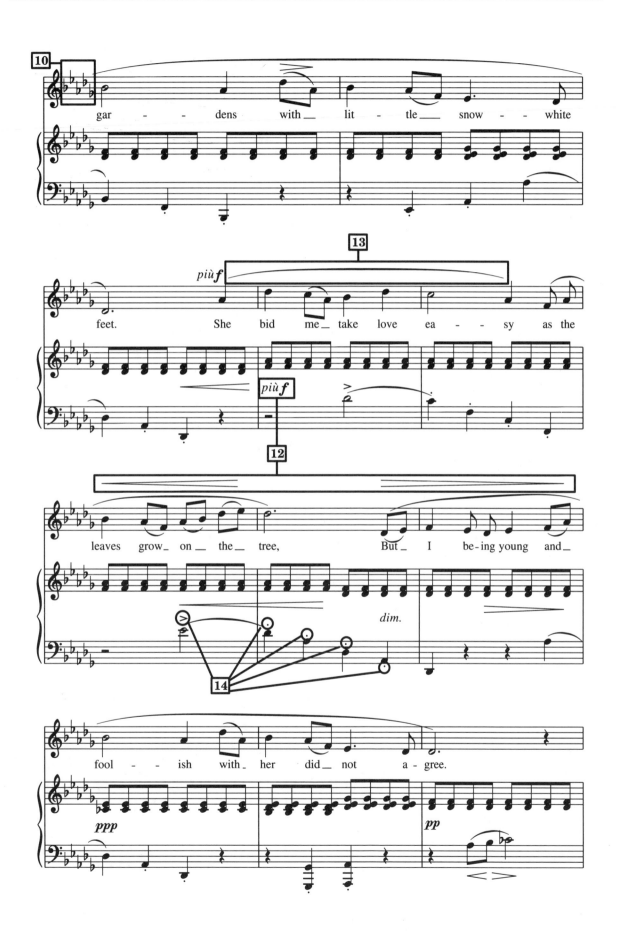

4. Bass Clef

The piano line uses another clef as well, the *bass clef (𝄢)*. Singers also use the bass clef, and it is associated with pitches sung by changed, male voices. All the vocal material in the *We Will Sing!* Performance Projects uses treble voices notated in the treble clef.

5. The Musical Staff

Pitches are arranged on a series of lines and spaces, grouped in ways that organize the written page. These lines and spaces are known as a *staff*. Notice the clef signs are drawn over all five lines and four spaces.

6. Bar Line

The staff is separated by vertical black lines called *bar lines*. Bar lines occur in direct relationship to the *meter signature*.

7. Meter Signature

This numerical indication alerts the musician to the groupings of beats in the works (refer to Practice Project Six for more detail). In this instance, the top number indicates four beats to each measure. The bar lines, then, will occur every four beats.

8. Measure

The spaces between the bar lines are known as *measures*. Music sometimes comes with the measures numbered for easy reference, which is particularly useful when rehearsing a piece of music. Starting at the top left corner, try numbering all the measures from the beginning to the end of the example.

9. System

A *system* is a set of staves connected by a line and/or brackets. In the example given, there are three staves in each system.

10. Key Signature

The beginning of each system shows other important information to the musician. The *key signature,* occurring directly before the meter signature, establishes the tonality of a piece. Tonal music is written by grouping certain pitches. The key signature tells the musician which group of pitches will be used in a given musical work. Britten's arrangement of *The Sally Gardens* makes use of five flats indicating the piece will sound in the key of D♭ major. (Refer to Practice Project Seven for more detail.)

11. Tempo Markings

The speed at which a musical work will go depends greatly on the *tempo marking,* located directly above the time signature. The marking can occur as a word, in this case *Commodo,* or as a number ($\♩$ = 66). The words are frequently in a foreign language, most often Italian. These words describe the character of a piece. As a tempo marking, the Italian term *Commodo* means flowing or easy. This information, combined with the numerical information, clues the musician into the speed and character of the piece.

12. Dynamics

The use of *dynamics* indicates the degree of loudness the composer intends. Dynamic markings fall in the following ranges from softest to loudest:

pianissimo	*piano*	*mezzo-piano*	*mezzo-forte*	*forte*	*fortissimo*

very soft	*soft*	*medium-soft*	*medium-loud*	*loud*	*very loud*

Dynamics should be regarded as a rich palette of choices which include the barely audible to the very fullest tone. As mentioned earlier, the written score is only a rough approximation of the composer's intentions. This is especially true with regard to dynamics. One musician's definition of loud might be considerably different than another's. How then does the musician make the appropriate choice? One must take into account all the other elements discussed in this project. For example, having learned that *The Sally Gardens* is relaxed and easy, at a relatively slow tempo, how would you expect the forte marking (*f*) at m.12 to sound in relationship to the text, tempo, and other dynamic indications?

Dynamics can also be indicated as a change from one degree of loudness to another. Consider the *crescendo/decrescendo* marking below:

13. Phrase Markings

Another important indication is the phrase and/or slur markings. The *phrase mark* or *legato* indication is a solid line connecting groups of notes together to indicate an important grouping with no separation of sound. The most obvious phrase mark might occur from the beginning to the end of a sentence, completing a thought. Find an example of a phrase mark in *The Sally Gardens* that encompasses a full sentence.

14. Articulation

A *slur mark* functions much like the phrase or legato indication as it requires the musician to connect groups of pitches together. The slur mark, however, can group together small numbers of pitches, or much larger groupings of pitches, and may not be related at all to the text. Find an example of a *two-note slur* marking in the musical example.

Finally, a composer can use various means of *articulation* to exact specific means of attack and decay of sounds. For example, a *staccato* marking indicates a detached sound. Find an example of a slur mark followed by a staccato mark in the piano line of the musical example.

Performance Practice

Once the above terms have been identified in a musical work, the musician can delve even further into the score. A closer examination will reveal the composer's intentions regarding performance of the work. It is important to keep in mind that composers of this century are especially careful to notate on the written page what the performers are to consider when making musical decisions about a piece.

This was not always true in earlier centuries however. A knowledge of the specific performance practices of the time becomes important in the absence of written notation. This knowledge comes from both study and practical experience. Like reading the score, knowledge of performance practice requires a continual refinement of skills, occurring even at the most advanced level of musicianship. Yet, even the youngest musician can participate in the process of determining musical style.

Interpretation

Once the musician is oriented to the written notation, the many indications in the score serve as a foundation for making decisions about how to perform the piece, and also how to interpret the piece. Within the context of the larger structure or form, these many markings have a specific purpose for which the musician takes the responsibility to produce, practice, and perform. Alongside learning to use your singing voice skillfully and interpreting the composer's notation, reading music is a powerful skill in the process of developing overall musicianship.

Summary

Following the score becomes a journey in discovering *relationships*. Understanding written notation is the first step toward interpreting the music. However, musical understanding develops from the ability to examine the relationships between *all* elements of the written score. To begin your journey of discovery, **identify** recurring patterns, **discuss** the function of the text, **compare** dynamics from section to section, **examine** relationships between key signatures and meter changes, **compare** phrase structure and articulation markings!

Selected Recordings

We Will Sing! cassette, side 2. *The Sally Gardens,* Sara, age 12, soloist, accompanied by William Buhr.

Another solo performance has been recorded by English tenor Robert Tear.

Folksong Arrangements. Robert Tear, tenor; Philip Ledger, piano. EMI CDM7 69423-2.

You may also enjoy listening to a traditional Irish performance of the folksong *The Sally Gardens,* performed by the Irish group "Clanad."

Clanad in Concert. Shanachie 79030.

Practice Project Five

M Y   P E R F O R M A N C E   P O R T F O L I O

Problem-Solving Exercises

Name:_____ Date:_____

Identify and **number** the following musical notation in the choral score of *She's Like the Swallow*. Use the *Sally Gardens* illustration in Practice Project Five as a model. Fill in the blanks on the score from the list of terms below:

1) text

2) vocal line

3) instrumental line

4) treble clef

5) bass clef

6) staff

7) bar line

8) time signature

9) measure

10) system

11) key signature

12) tempo indication

13) mezzo-piano

14) crescendo

15) phrase mark

Practice Project Six

Feeling Time and Reading Rhythm

In the next two practice projects you will have the opportunity to develop your music reading skills. The ability to read music and perform accurately is an important part of your musicianship. Practice Project Six begins with feeling time and reading rhythm. You will learn to: (1) feel the pulse; (2) identify the meter of musical works; (3) conduct beat patterns; and (4) read rhythm. Follow the directions in each section and review this material regularly.

As you prepare to sing the opening of Aaron Copland's *Ching-a-ring Chaw,* tap your toe in time with the bass notes of the piano accompaniment. Just as our heart beats a pulse in our body, most music has an underlying pulse or beat. This is what we feel when we tap our toe or snap our fingers "in time with the music."

Ex. 1. Ching-a-Ring Chaw
We Will Sing! cassette, side 2

Meter and Meter Signatures

The many beats in *Ching-a-ring Chaw* are grouped in two's. Each measure contains two beats. Look at the beginning of the *Ching-a-ring Chaw* excerpt above. The numbers ²₄ are called the *meter signature.* The top number "2" tells you that there are two beats or pulses in each measure. **Identify** the other songs in Performance Project Program One which organize the music in groups of two beats per measure.

The grouping of beats is called *meter.* When the music is organized in groups of two beats per measure we say that the music is in *duple meter.* The next example is different.

Bist du bei mir by J.S. Bach is written in *triple meter* because the music is organized in groups of three beats per measure. Again, the top number "3" tells you that there are three beats or pulses in each measure. **Identify** the other songs in Performance Project Program One which organize the music in groups of three beats per measure.

Listen to the recorded example of *Bist du bei mir* (*We Will Sing!* cassette, side 2). Follow the excerpt and answer the following questions. (1) How does the ¾ meter signature of *Bist du bei mir* help us identify that the music is arranged in triple meter? (2) Is there another way of learning that the music is organized in triple meter?

Ex. 2. Bist du bei mir
We Will Sing! cassette side 2

Conducting Time

We need to know the meter of a musical work in order to practice and perform the music. Each meter can be shown through movement activities such as clapping the beats or conducting time.

Duple Meter

The Irish folk song, *I Know Where I'm Goin'* is organized in duple meter as shown in Ex. 3. Can you identify the meter signature? **Sing** this short excerpt thinking about how the music moves in groups of two beats per measure.

Ex. 3. I Know Where I'm Goin'

Using the two-pattern suggested in Ex. 4, **conduct** time to *I Know Where I'm Goin'*.

Ex. 4. Conducting Pattern in 2

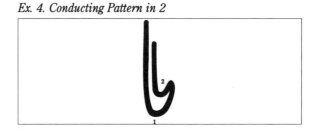

Triple Meter

Bist du bei mir is organized in triple meter as shown in Ex. 5. Can you identify this meter signature?

Sing this excerpt, thinking about how the music moves in groups of three beats per measure.

 Ex. 5. Bist du bei mir
We Will Sing! cassette, side 2

 Listen to *Bist du bei mir* (*We Will Sing!* cassette, side 2), and **practice** conducting this excerpt of *Bist du bei mir* using the suggested three-pattern in Ex. 6.

Ex. 6. Conducting Pattern in 3

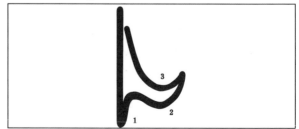

Conducting in 4

Benjamin Britten's *The Sally Gardens* has a meter signature of ⁴⁄₄ as shown in Ex. 7.

Sing this short excerpt thinking about how the music moves in groups of four beats per measure.

Ex. 7. The Sally Gardens
We Will Sing! cassette, side 2

Since 4 is a multiple of 2, this work is also considered an example of *duple meter*. The conducting pattern for music feeling in four is given in Ex. 8. **Practice** conducting this excerpt using the illustrated four-pattern.

Ex. 8. Conducting Pattern in 4

Compound Meter

The musical excerpts you have practiced were in *simple duple* and *simple triple* meter. The meter signature helped you choose which conducting pattern to use. Look at this excerpt from *The Path to the Moon*. Notice that the meter signature is §. **Sing** this short excerpt to determine how many beats you feel per measure.

Ex. 9. The Path to the Moon
We Will Sing! cassette, side 2

Look again at Ex. 9. The top number of the meter signature indicates that there are six beats per measure. **Listen** to *The Path to the Moon* (*We Will Sing!* cassette, side 2) and **practice** conducting using the suggested six-pattern given in Ex. 10.

Ex. 10. Conducting Pattern in 6

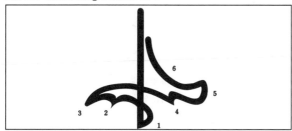

If you conduct every one of the six beats, this song loses its sustained, lyrical quality. **Sing** the excerpt swaying gently from side to side, feeling

only two pulses per measure. **Sing** the excerpt again conducting the music using the two-pattern learned from Ex. 4. Feeling § compound meter in two pulses gives a lilting, lyrical quality to the piece. **Identify** other pieces in § from the music in Performance Project Program Two.

Oliver Cromwell is also an example of § compound meter felt and conducted in two. **Listen** to the recorded example of *Oliver Cromwell* (*We Will Sing!* cassette, side 2) and **conduct** the music using the two-pattern shown in Ex. 4.

 Ex. 11. Oliver Cromwell
We Will Sing! cassette, side 2

The time indications §, ⁹⁄₈, and ¹²⁄₈ are all examples of *compound meter*. Unless the music moves very slowly, § is usually conducted in two as shown in Ex. 4. ⁹⁄₈ is most often conducted in three as shown in Ex. 6. ¹²⁄₈ is usually conducted in four as shown in Ex. 8.

 Handel's song "How Beautiful are the Feet of Them" is an example of ¹²⁄₈ compound meter felt in four. **Listen** to the recorded example of Handel's song (*We Will Sing!* cassette, side 2) and follow the score in Performance Project Program Three. **Conduct** the time while you listen, using the four-pattern.

Other Meters

Jingle Bell Swing has a meter signature of $\frac{5}{4}$. There are five beats in each measure. Find the beat, snap in time with the music, then **conduct** the opening of *Jingle Bell Swing* using the five-pattern shown in Ex. 13.

Ex. 13. Conducting Pattern for 5

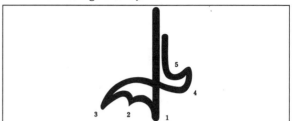

Ex. 12. Jingle Bell Swing
We Will Sing! cassette, side 2

You may also find examples of music organized in groups of 7, 10, 11, or even 13. Music in one of these meters may be conducted using combinations of beat patterns. You will learn more about other meter patterns in *We Will Sing!*, Books Two and Three.

Free Meter

Look at the opening of this excerpt from Benjamin Britten's *A Ceremony of Carols*. There is no meter signature to help us identify the meter. "Hodie" is an example of *plainsong style*. Each group of pitches is organized by the natural meter of the text. Every measure of music has its own meter and is conducted in a combination of patterns. **Sing** and **conduct** the different patterns found in "Hodie" shown in Ex. 14.

Ex 14. "Hodie" from A Ceremony of Carols
We Will Sing! cassette, side 2

Reading Rhythm

Chant the words *"Ching-a-ring-a-ring ching chaw."* Did you notice that some sounds were short and some were long? This combination of short and long sounds is called *rhythm.* **Clap** the rhythm of the first line of *Ching-a-ring Chaw* as shown in Ex. 15.

Ex. 15. Ching-a-ring Chaw

Ching-a- ring-a ring ching chaw

Practice clapping these rhythms:

Ex. 16.

You are now beginning to read rhythm. The next section will help you develop and improve your rhythm skills.

Using Words

In vocal music, composers often use the rhythm of the words, or the "way the words go" for the rhythm patterns of the song. Chanting the words will help you know how the rhythm sounds. Try these exercises:

(a) **Chant** the text:

Ex. 17. Simple Gifts

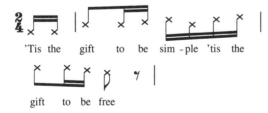

'Tis the gift to be sim -ple 'tis the

gift to be free

(b) **Clap** the rhythm without text:

Ex. 18.

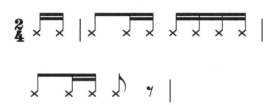

(c) **Chant** the text:

Ex. 19. Oliver Cromwell

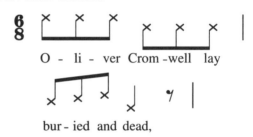

O - li - ver Crom -well lay

bur - ied and dead,

(d) **Clap** the rhythm:

Ex. 20.

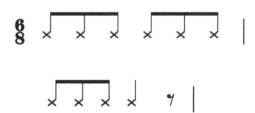

In each of these examples the words and rhythms fit exactly. The *composed rhythm* mirrors the *natural rhythm* of the words.

In instrumental music, as well as more complex vocal music, words may be unavailable as a way to guide the performer rhythmically. In such cases, the musician must read the rhythms independently of words. There are several ways to read rhythm in music without words. Two different systems are shown next.

Using the Metric System

The metric system is particularly useful when the rhythm is complex, or when the music being learned is in a foreign language. Counting with metric syllables helps the singer feel time. In *Bist du bei mir,* for example, the text "Bist du bei mir" is set with two different rhythm patterns as shown in Ex. 21a and 21b.

Chanting the natural rhythm of the text will not help here. We need another way to read these rhythms. Singing on numbers will help you learn to feel inner pulse and read rhythm.

Identify what you already know about this piece. The meter signature is ¾. This means that there are three beats per bar. **Listen** to your teacher play the piano accompaniment. **Sing** the vocal line using the numbers shown in Ex. 22.[1] (You may prefer to listen to the recorded performance on the *We Will Sing!* cassette, side 2)

Ex. 21a and b. Bist du bei mir

Ex. 22. Bist du bei mir

---

1   Note: When using the metric system, the syllable "ti" may be substituted for the word "three". This syllable modification is easier to produce, and the results are more precise.

Look at m. 3 in Ex. 22. The note on each beat is called a *quarter note*(♩). Find other quarter notes in this Bach excerpt. Notice that in mm. 5 and 6 there are two notes for every beat. These are called *eighth notes*. As you can see, they can be written singly (♪) or in pairs (♫). Using the metric system, count the pattern shown in Ex. 23.

Ex. 23. Bist du bei mir

The rhythm pattern shown in Ex. 24 also has two notes per beat, but they look and sound different. The dot after the first eighth note makes it longer (♪.). The shorter second note is called a *sixteenth note*. Sixteenth notes can be written singly, (♬) in pairs, (♬) or in groups of four, (♬♬).

Using the metric system, we can count the pattern shown in Ex. 24 like this:

Ex. 24. Bist du bei mir

Identify the pair of sixteenth notes shown in Ex. 22. When there are sixteenth notes in the rhythm of a piece, you can divide the beat by counting 1 ee and ah, 2 ee and ah, 3 ee and ah. **Sing** *Bist du bei mir* using the metric system.

In works organized in ⁶⁄₈, such as *The Path to the Moon,* we can sing the numbers "1 - 2 - 3 - 4 - 5 - 6", or "1 & 2 & 3 & 4 & 5 & 6 &".

Sing the excerpt from *The Path to the Moon,* shown in Ex. 25. Use the metric system to help you feel pulse and read rhythm.

Ex. 25. The Path to the Moon

Counting Rests

Rests symbolize musical silence. You must learn to think in time but not to sing or play through rests. When using the metric system to feel pulse and read rhythm, *think,* but do not *sing* when you see a rest.

Sing the following excerpt from Dmitri Kabalevsky's *Good Night.* **Think, tap,** or **clap** the count whenever a rest occurs.

Ex. 26. Good Night

Using Rhythm Syllables

Another way of reading rhythm is to sing or chant "rhythm syllables." For example: the rhythmic pattern from the last four measures of the *Good Night* excerpt in Ex. 26 could be chanted in the following manner:

Here are three different examples of rhythm syllables. Each of these patterns can be found in one of the musical works in this music text. **Chant** the syllables and **clap** the rhythms. **Identify** the song which uses each rhythm pattern shown in Ex. 27.

Ex. 27a, 27b, and 27c.

You may use the list shown in Ex. 28 as a glossary of rhythm syllables to help you perform rhythm patterns in your singing.

Ex. 28. Glossary of Rhythm Syllables

Rhythm notation	Rhythm syllable
♩	ta
♫	ti-ti
♩. ♪	ta-m-ti
♪ ♩.	ti-tam
♪ ♩ ♪	syn-co-pa
♪♪♪ (3)	tri-o-la
♬♬	ti-ka-ti-ka
♫♬	ti-ti-ka
♬♫	ti-ka-ti
♩.♪	tim-ka
♪♩.	tik-um
𝅗𝅥	ta-aa
𝅗𝅥.	ta-aa-aa
𝅝	ta-aa-aa-aa

Rests: (Syllables are "thought" not sung or chanted)

Ex. 29. Glossary of Rhythm Syllables (Rests)

Rhythm notation	Rhythm syllable
𝄽	sa
𝄾	si
𝄼	sa-aa
𝄼.	sa-aa-aa
𝄻	sa-aa-aa-aa

Which syllables would you use for this excerpt from *Good Night?* **Sing** the short excerpt shown in Ex. 30 with rhythm syllables.

Ex. 30. Good Night

Syncopation

Listen to the recorded performance of the excerpt of *Oliver Cromwell* shown in Ex. 31 (We Will Sing! cassette, side 2). You will notice that the accented words fall regularly on the first beat of each measure. The vocal rhythm starting at m. 9 occurs "on the beat." **Listen** to the recorded example and **clap** the accents in each measure.

Ex. 31. Oliver Cromwell

Sing this well-known holiday song shown in Ex. 32. Be sure to **clap** and **sing** the accents where you see the accent sign (>).

You will notice that like the song *Oliver Cromwell,* the accent falls regularly on beat one of each measure.

Ex. 32. Jingle Bells (traditional)

Dash - ing through the   snow   in a   one horse o - pen   sleigh

Listen to the short jazz version of *Jingle Bell Swing* (*We Will Sing!* cassette, side 2). This arrangement uses accents on the normally weak beats 4 and 5, and rhythm patterns which shift the rhythm "off the beat." **Clap** the accents in each measure shown in Ex. 33.

Ex. 33. Jingle Bell Swing

Dash-ing   through the snow   in a   one horse   o - pen sleigh   O'er the   fields we go

Laugh- ing   all   the way.   Bells   on   bob   tails ring,   O ____

Chant this example of syncopated rhythm shown in Ex. 34.

Ex 34. Jingle Bell Swing

Dash - ing   through   the snow   in a   one horse   o - pen sleigh

Did you feel the accents and rhythm patterns differently than in the traditional version of *Jingle Bells? Syncopation* is created in *Jingle Bell Swing* by placing an eighth note rest (𝄾) on beat 2, followed by a quarter note (♩).

Sing the excerpt from *Jingle Bell Swing,* shown in Ex. 35. **Tap** the beat. **Identify** the syncopated rhythms. Syncopation is an important feature of jazz but may also be found in many other styles of music.

Ex. 35. Jingle Bell Swing

Dash-ing through the snow in a   one horse   o - pen sleigh   O'er the   fields we go

Laugh-ing   all   the way.   Bells   on   bob   tails ring,   O ____

Summary

In Practice Project Six you have learned to feel the beat in music and to perform the beat through clapping and conducting. You have also learned several different systems to help you read and perform rhythm. Now that you have learned the principles of reading rhythm, you will have the opportunity to exercise your skills in performing choral music. Review *Practice Project Six* as often as you like to continue improving your musicianship. The skills necessary to perform and enjoy choral music will develop if you regularly exercise these counting and reading systems.

M Y P E R F O R M A N C E P O R T F O L I O

Problem-Solving Exercises

Name: _____ Date: _____

1. For practice identifying meter and conducting time, look at the musical works in Performance Project Program One.

   a) **Identify** the meter.

   b) **Choose** the appropriate conducting pattern for each piece.

   c) Using the *We Will Sing!* cassette, or a recording of your choir, **conduct** one of the works from Performance Project Program One.

2. For practice with the metric system, **clap** and **count** the following rhythm patterns while singing these excerpts from Bach's *Bist du bei mir*.

3. **Clap** and **count** these rhythm patterns while singing this excerpt from Copland's *Simple Gifts*.

4. For practice using rhythm syllables, **sing** the following excerpt from Copland's *Simple Gifts*. Use the glossary of Rhythm Syllables in *Practice Project Six,* to help you choose appropriate syllables.

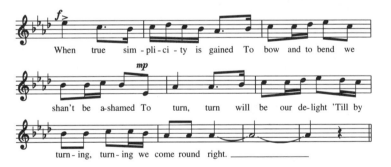

Practice Project Seven
Hearing Pitch and Reading Notation

In this practice project you will have the opportunity to further develop your music reading ability. Practice Project Seven concentrates on hearing pitch and reading notation. You will learn to: (1) sing solfa; (2) use handsigns to show pitch; (3) identify major and minor tonalities; and (4) read and perform intervals accurately. Follow the directions for each section and review this material regularly.

Musical sounds can be high or low. The high and low of music is called *pitch*. Composers use patterns of pitch to create melody. Complete the following exercises.

Sing *Jubilate Deo* shown in Ex. 1.

Ex. 1. Jubilate Deo
We Will Sing! cassette, side 1

Ju – bi – la – te De – o. Ju – bi – la – te De – o. Al – le – lu – ia!

Notice that these pitches move up, in an *ascending* pattern, then move down in a *descending* pattern toward the final "Alleluia" section. Sometimes pitches move in stepwise motion. This is called *conjunct* movement. **Sing** the example of conjunct movement shown in Ex. 2.

Ex. 2. Jubilate Deo

Ju – bi – la –

Pitches may also move by leap. This is called *disjunct* movement. **Sing** the example of disjunct movement shown in Ex. 3.

Ex. 3. Jubilate Deo

Al – le – lu – ia!

Sometimes pitches repeat. **Sing** Ex. 3 once more noticing the repeated pitches in the middle of the word "Al-<u>le</u>-<u>lu</u>-ia."

The melody of *Oliver Cromwell* is also a combination of different kinds of pitch movement. **Sing** the short excerpt shown in Ex. 4. **Identify** (a) conjunct movement, (b) disjunct movement, and (c) repeated pitch. **Describe** the ascending and descending patterns you find in Ex. 4.

Ex. 4. Oliver Cromwell

As you have discovered by singing *Jubilate Deo*, pitch is written on a set of five lines with four spaces in between. Composers communicate their ideas by using the *musical staff* to organize pitch and time. **Identify** the five lines and four spaces shown in Ex. 5.

Ex. 5. The Musical Staff

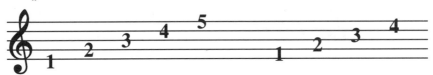

Using Tonic Solfa

One tool that musicians use to read music is called *tonic solfa.* Tonic solfa uses syllables to represent pitch. The first set of syllables to learn is shown in the diagram in Ex. 6.

Notice that there is a *do* at the bottom, and another *do'* at the top. Musicians use the symbol (') to show that the *do'* at the top sounds an octave higher. Often the solfa syllables are written using only the first letter of each syllable, as shown in the diagram in Ex. 7. **Sing** these solfa syllables beginning with low *do*.

Ex 6. Tonic Solfa Syllables

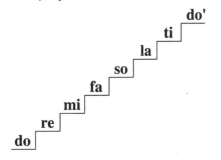

Ex 7. Tonic Solfa Syllables (letters only)

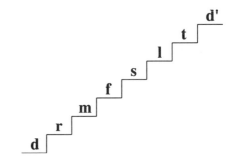

Sing *Jubilate Deo* with the solfa syllables written below the musical staff shown in Ex. 8.

Ex 8. Jubilate Deo

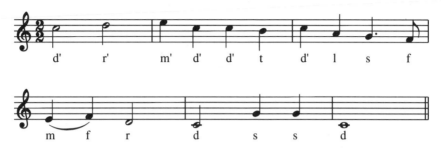

d'　r'　m'　d'　d'　t　d'　l　s　f

m　f　r　d　s　s　d

Curwen-Kodály Handsigns

There are also handsigns that represent solfa syllables. Look at the chart shown in Ex. 9 and **sing** *Jubilate Deo* shown in Ex. 8 while using the handsigns.

Ex 9. The Curwen-Kodály Handsigns for Solfege

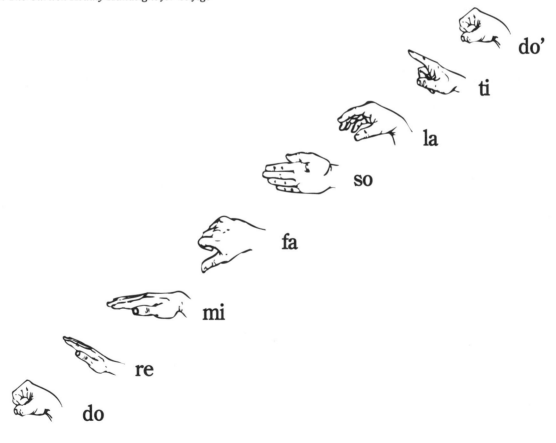

Major Tonality

Sing *Jubilate Deo,* using solfa syllables and **identify** where *do* is written on the staff.

Ex 10. Jubilate Deo

Sing *O Music,* using solfa syllables and **identify** where *do* is written on the staff.

Ex 11. O Music, Sweet Music

Sing *Simple Gifts,* using solfa syllables and **identify** where *do* is written on the staff.

Ex 12. Simple Gifts

In *Jubilate Deo, do'* is written on the third space of the staff:

Ex 13.

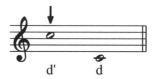

In *O Music, do* is on the second line:

Ex 14.

In *Simple Gifts, do* is on the second space:

Ex 15.

Making Scales

do is in a different place for each of these songs because each piece is written in a different major key (see Exs. 13, 14, and 15). An easy way to learn about keys is to look at a piano keyboard.

See the diagram shown in Ex. 16. If we start on the key marked *do* and play and sing all of the white notes to *do'*, we will have played and sung a major scale.

Ex 16. A Piano Keyboard

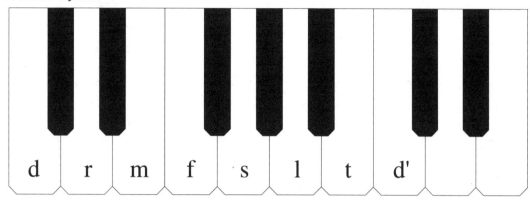

At the Keyboard

The piano keyboard has white notes and black notes. If we start on another key, we will need to include some black keys in our scale to make it

sound like a major scale. Look at Ex. 17. You will notice that *mi* (m) and *ti* (t) are played on black keys.

Ex 17.

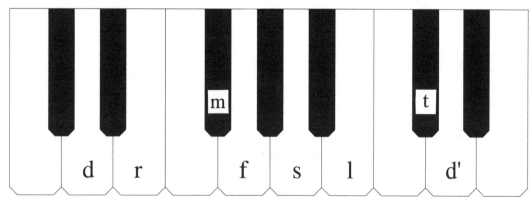

Scales are made up of combinations of whole-steps and half-steps.

Look at the chart shown below for the pattern of whole-steps and half-steps in a major scale:

Ex 18. Major Scale

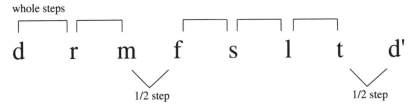

On the keyboard you can play half-steps by playing keys that are right next to each other.

Identify some half-steps on the keyboard shown in Ex. 19.

Ex. 19. Whole Steps and Half Steps on the Keyboard

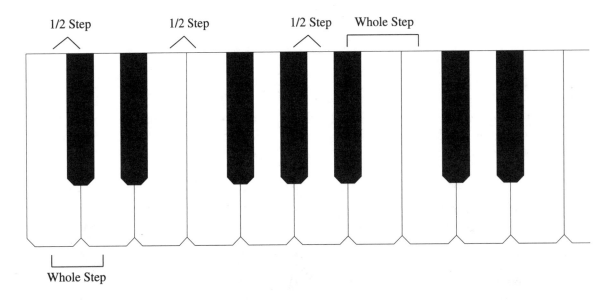

Whole-steps equal two half-steps. **Identify** two different patterns of whole-steps identified on the keyboard shown in Ex. 19.

Can you find other whole-step patterns on this keyboard?

Absolute Pitch Names

Each note on the piano keyboard corresponds to a pitch on the musical staff. The *absolute* names of these notes follow a musical "alphabet" "A - B - C - D - E - F - G". Look at the keyboard shown in Ex. 20 to find the *absolute* name of the pitches on the staff, beginning with middle C.

Ex. 20. Pitch Names

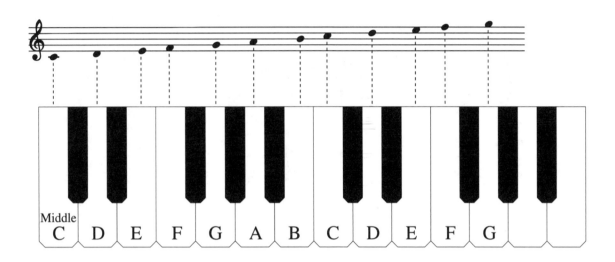

Look again at the major scale beginning on "C." If *do* is on C, the pattern of whole-steps and half-steps is created by playing only the white keys.

Ex. 21. C Major Scale

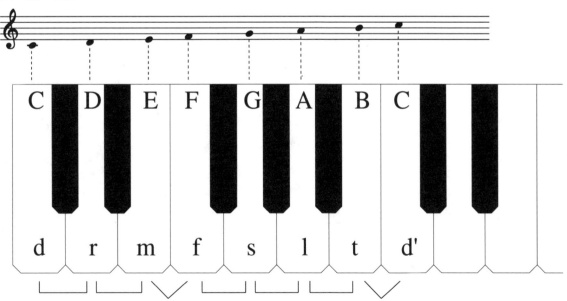

If you begin on any pitch other than C, you will need to play a combination of white and black keys in order to create the major scale pattern of whole-steps and half-steps. In Ex. 22, *do* is on D. To create the major scale pattern of whole-steps and half-steps you need to use two black keys.

Ex. 22. D Major Scale

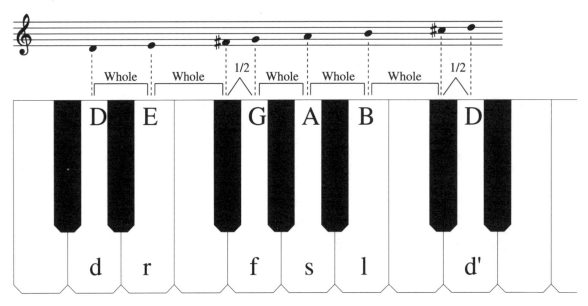

Black notes may be shown on the staff by adding a special sign next to the note. A sharp sign (♯) tells you to play or sing the note one half-step higher. A flat sign (♭) tells you to play or sing the note one half-step lower. **Name** the black notes shown on the keyboard and staff in Ex. 23.

Ex. 23. Sharps and Flats

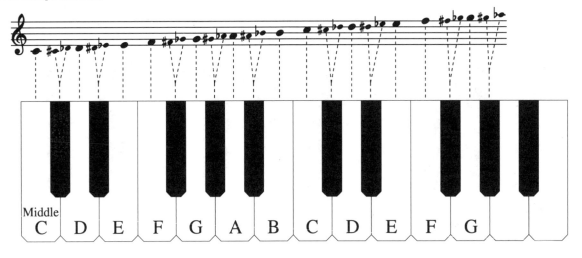

Finding Do

Find the sharp sign (♯) at the beginning of *O Music* in Ex. 24. This notation is called a *key signature*. The key signature at the beginning of a written score tells you which sharps (♯) or which flats (♭) to play or sing throughout the piece.

Ex 24. O Music

O — mu - sic, sweet,

If you are going to read music using solfa, you must first find *do*. The key signature will help you to find *do*. Remember these two rules:

Rule #1

If the key signature indicates sharps(♯), the last sharp is *ti*. To find *do*, count down *ti, la, so, fa, mi, re, do,* as shown in Ex. 25.

Ex 25.

t   l   s   f   m   r   d

Rule #2

If the key signature indicates flats (♭), the last flat is *fa*. To find *do*, count down *fa, mi, re, do,* as shown in Ex. 26.

Ex 26.

f   m   r   d

Using the rules given above, find *do* in each of the following works:

1. O Music, Sweet Music

2. Sally Gardens

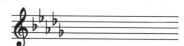

3. Ching-a-ring Chaw

4. Spring Morning

Minor Tonality

Not all music is written in major tonality. **Sing** the melody of Dmitri Kabalevsky's *Good Night* with the solfa syllables written below the staff as shown in Ex. 27.

Ex 27. Good Night

Good Night is written using notes from the *minor scale* as shown in Ex. 28. The minor scale begins on the syllable *la.*

Sing the minor scale which forms the tonal basis for *Good Night.* Use the solfa syllables written below the staff shown in Ex. 28.

Ex 28. d minor scale

Pitch Alterations – Accidentals

The Canadian folk song *She's Like the Swallow* is written in a minor tonality. In Ex. 29, notice the *natural sign* (♮) in m. 11. Many times composers use notes from other tonalities. These "borrowed" notes are shown in the music with sharps (♯), flats (♭), or natural (♮) signs. When these signs are used in the music next to a pitch they are called *accidentals.* Accidentals change the name of the solfa syllable. In *She's Like the Swallow,* the natural sign (♮) in measure eleven raises the syllable from *fa* to *fi.* **Sing** the first verse with the solfa syllables written below the staff shown in Ex. 29.

Ex. 29. She's Like the Swallow

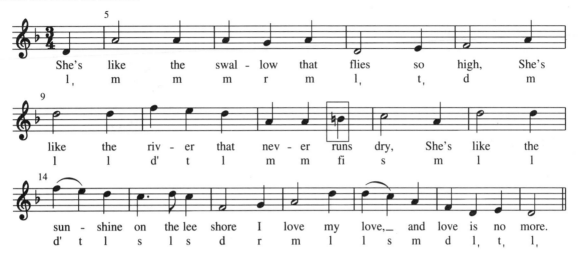

She's like the swal - low that flies so high, She's
l, m m m r m l, t, d m

like the riv - er that nev - er runs dry, She's like the
l l d' t l m m fi s m l l

sun - shine on the lee shore I love my love,_ and love is no more.
d' t l s l s d r m l l s m d l, t, l,

Chromatic Syllables and Handsigns

The melody for *Bist du bei mir* includes four different *accidentals*.

1. **Sing** each of the following examples using solfa syllables.

Ex. 30. Bist du bei mir

s d r' t   d f f f m s t s fi s

Without the accidental, the note in m. 5 would be called *fa*. Because the sharp sign (♯) raises the pitch one half-step, it is called *fi*. **Practice** the handsign for *fi* shown in Ex. 31.

Ex. 31. Handsign for fi

Sing the solfa syllables and **sign** the excerpt from *Bist du bei mir* in Ex. 30.

2.   Sing Ex. 32 using solfa syllables.

Ex. 32. Bist du bei mir

d'   m'   d'   ta   l   l

The fourth note in m. 10 would be called *ti,* but the flat sign (♭) lowers the pitch one half-step, changing its name to *ta.*

Practice the handsign for *ta* shown in Ex. 33.

Ex. 33. Handsign for ta

Sing the solfa syllables and **sign** the excerpt in Ex. 32.

3.   Sing Ex. 34 using solfa syllables.

Ex. 34. Bist du bei mir

l   d'   l   si   l   m   l   d'   l   si   l   r   di   r   t   d'r'   d'   t   l   t   m   si   l

a)   The fourth note in m. 23 would be *so,* but the sharp sign (♯) raises it to *si.* Notice the difference between the handsign for *so* and the handsign for *si.*   **Practice** the hand-signs for *so* and *si* shown in Ex. 35.

Ex. 35. Handsigns for so and si

b)   The second note in m. 25 in Ex. 34 would be *do,* but the sharp sign (♯) raises it one half-step to *di.* **Practice** changing the angle of your hand to show the difference between *do* and *di* as shown in Ex. 36.

Ex. 36. Handsigns for do and di

Sing the solfa syllables and **sign** the entire excerpt from *Bist du bei mir* shown in Ex. 34 concentrating on the accidentals.

Intervals

At the beginning of Practice Project Seven, we learned that pitches could repeat or move in *conjunct* or *disjunct* motion. The distance between two pitches is called an *interval*.

Major Intervals

Using tonic solfa is one way to help singers remember how a specific interval sounds. Intervals are given number names to describe the distance between the two pitches. When naming intervals, count both the bottom and the top pitches. **Sing** these major and perfect intervals, beginning on *do:*

Ex. 38. Major and Perfect Intervals

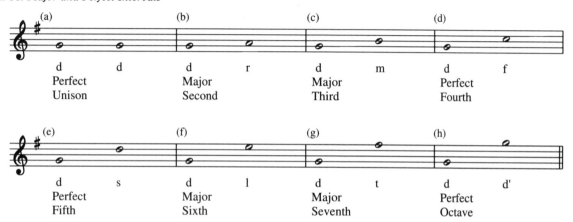

Notice that the unison, fourth, fifth, and octave intervals are called *perfect* intervals. The other intervals shown in Ex. 38 are called *major* intervals.

Minor Intervals

Some intervals have a minor quality. **Sing** the following minor intervals with solfa syllables as indicated in Ex. 39.

Ex 39. Minor Intervals

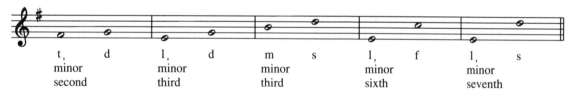

Minor intervals are one half-step smaller than major intervals. Look at these major and minor intervals on the keyboard, shown in Ex. 40.

Ex 40. Intervals on the Keyboard

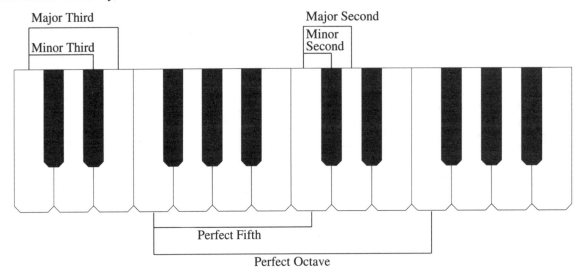

Summary

In Practice Project Seven you have learned to read pitch on a musical staff using solfa syllables and handsigns. You have also learned about different kinds of intervals including major, minor, and perfect. The ability to recognize and perform intervals will help you sing with musicianship.

These reading skills are the basic tools for performing music artistically. Now that you have learned the principles of reading music, you will have the opportunity to exercise your skills in performing choral music. **Review** this Practice Project regularly to improve your reading skills. The skill necessary to perform choral music will develop if you regularly practice singing solfa and interval recognition.

Practice Project Seven

M Y P E R F O R M A N C E P O R T F O L I O

Problem-Solving Exercises

Name:_____ Date:_____

1. Using the music reading guidelines found in *Practice Project Seven*, **find** *do* in each of the following works from *Performance Project Program Two*. Write on the staff provided.

   (a) I Know Where I'm Goin'

   (b) Ching-a-ring Chaw

   (c) The Path to the Moon

   (d) Oliver Cromwell

2. **Sing** *A Child is Born* with text. Using the key signature as a guide, **find** *do* and **mark** the solfa syllables below the staff.

A Child is Born

For us a child is born this day, No - well _____

_____ no - well, no - well, no - well, no - well.

3. **Sing** the following excerpt from *Bist du bei mir* and **identify** and **name** the intervals highlighted here.

Bist du bei mir

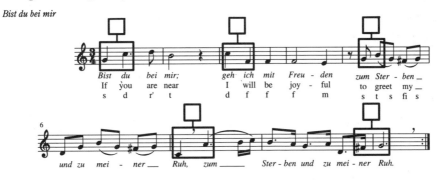

Bist du bei mir; geh ich mit Freu - den zum Ster - ben _
If you are near I will be joy - ful to greet my _
s d r' t   d f f f m   s t s fis s

und zu mei - ner _ Ruh, zum _____ Ster - ben und zu mei - ner Ruh.

PART 4

Singing Together

Part 4

Singing Together

Part 4 introduces the musical repertoire. Grouped into three distinct Performance Projects, each Program includes six varied compositions, along with detailed musical orientations and optional rehearsal guides. This versatile formatting makes it possible for the classroom teacher or the music specialist to use the materials in a variety of different ways. While the classroom teacher may find the rehearsal guidelines essential in teaching the repertoire, the music specialist may prefer to use the repertoire independently of the rehearsal guide, teaching through an alternative pedagogy.

The rehearsal activities in *We Will Sing!* are constructed in such a way that some students may work independently or in small ensemble groups. However they are used, the rehearsal guidelines are developed to encourage a positive musical experience, one that necessarily revolves around classroom singing, develops the student's musicianship, and culminates in musical enjoyment and self-growth.

Each musical work is contextualized by an "Orientation" which details the musical elements, form, and style of the composition along with a short social-historical profile. The teacher-conductor should use the orientation information in context of the lesson-rehearsal as an opportunity to enhance the development of musicianship rather than using it separately to teach a lesson *about* the music. The "Rehearsal Guides" develop sequentially beginning with the opportunity to: *(a) produce* the music through singing; *(b) practice* the musicianship necessary to meet the musical challenges; and *(c) perform* the music with skill and understanding. (For more detail concerning instruction, refer to *A Teaching Model for Classroom Choirs* in Part 1.)

Various methods of introducing the music are suggested depending on the length, character, and complexity of the composition. Through constant *musical doing* and consistent opportunities for *musical reflecting,* the sequential instruction encourages the development of musicianship and empowers students to succeed. Each lesson-rehearsal finishes with the opportunity to perform the work. The classroom performance must testify to the students' musical understanding. Successful performance is a form of *thinking-in-action* — knowledge that is demonstrated rather than described.

PERFORMANCE PROJECTS

Program One

Orientation

O Music, Sweet Music
Lowell Mason (1792 – 1872)

Pitch

Vocal Line: Conjunct stepwise motion developed around: *do - re - mi - fa - so*

Tonality: G major (Begins *do - re - mi*)

Phrase Structure: Three 4-bar phrases (4 + 4 + 4)

Texture: Unison song with piano accompaniment (optional canon version in three parts)

Vocal Range:

Time

Meter: Duple

Meter Signature: $\frac{2}{2}$

Conduct: In 2

Tempo: (♩ = ca. 112)

Characteristic Rhythm:

Performance Timing: ca. 2′ 30″

Text

Source: Lowell Mason

Theme: Festive school song celebrating music and inviting the chorus to sing.

Form

Unison version organized in three 4-bar phrases; may be sung in two- or three-part canon.

Style

19th century American school song written for the purpose of motivating and inspiring students to sing.

Social - Historical

Lowell Mason was America's first public school music teacher known for his ability in hymn singing and conducting choirs. In 1838, Mr. Mason convinced the Boston schools to include singing as an essential part of the school curriculum.

O MUSIC
VERSION 1
Unison Voices with Piano Accompaniment

LOWELL MASON
Arranged by Doreen Rao

O MUSIC
VERSION 2
Canon in two or three parts*

LOWELL MASON
Arranged by Doreen Rao

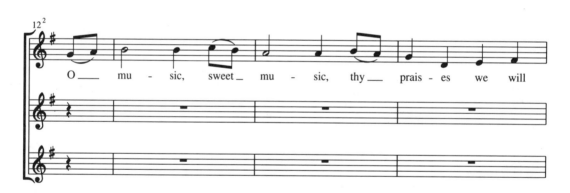

* The version in canon may be performed unaccompanied, or with the keyboard accompaniment of the unison version.

Rehearsal Guide

O Music, Sweet Music

> Your ability to perform *O Music, Sweet Music* requires musicianship. In rehearsal, you will have the opportunity to *produce* the song, *practice* the musicianship necessary to meet the musical challenges, and *perform* with skill and understanding.

The musical challenges of performing this song include your ability to:

- **sing** the ascending melody built on a major 3rd;

- **contrast** the sustained long note rhythms with the shorter eighth- and quarter-note rhythms;

- **sustain** the smooth legato line organized in three 4-bar phrases;

- **listen** and **support** the in-tune cadences at the end of each section.

Producing

1. Using your best posture, **sing** the melody *O Music, Sweet Music* (Version 1). Your teacher will guide you as you sing in unison with your choir.

Practicing

1. With the music in your hand, **follow your score** as your teacher conducts you through the whole song once more.

2. As you read the music, keep a tall, singing posture. Remember to hold the music high and look at your conductor while you are singing.

3. **Identify** how many different sections you heard.

4. **Sing** the first phrase (mm. 3-6). Did you notice that the ascending melody is built on a major third?

5. **Sing** the second phrase (mm. 6-10). Did you notice how the melody begins as an ascending five note scale to what we call the perfect fifth?

6. **Sing** the third phrase (mm. 11-14). Did you notice how the melodic and rhythmic character of the third phrase changes?

7. **Sing** both the first phrase and the second phrase with a good preparatory breath and supported *singing* tone. Be careful to avoid using the everyday speaking voice. **Describe** how the second phrase differs from the first phrase.

8. **Identify** the descending eighth-note *sequences* in the second phrase, then **sing** the whole 4-bar phrase with enough breath to support the highest note of the song. Point to the highest note in the score, and **name** the note.

9. **Sing** the whole song again in unison until you feel very secure and in control of the music. As you sing, be sure to **shape** the

(oo) [u] vowel in the word "music." *For a lesson in vocal phonetics, see Practice Project Four.*

10. When you feel ready and your unison singing is secure, begin rehearsing Lowell Mason's school song in 2-part, then 3-part canon (Version 2).

Performing

1. **Sing** the whole song in unison. Follow the conductor and remember to:

   • **begin** each musical phrase with a preparatory breath;

   • **sustain** the smooth legato phrases;

   • **support** the final pitch of each phrase so the cadences are sung in tune;

   • **communicate** the character of the words to express the idea of pleasure and praise.

Reflecting - Evaluating

You have been learning how to use your singing voice, you have been developing your music reading and counting skills, and you have been studying Lowell Mason's school song *O Music, Sweet Music.* In rehearsal, you *produced* the song with your singing voice, you *practiced* the musicianship required to meet the musical challenges, and you *performed* in class or concert. As you review your performance, complete the following reflections for your journal.

1. **Describe** how you used your voice to perform this song.

2. **Describe** your ability to meet the musical challenges in performing artistically.

3. **Describe** how you could improve your performance.

   • As an assessment alternative, you may complete the Performance Critique form to include in your *We Will Sing!* Performance Portfolio.

To improve your musicianship and to perform artistically, you may return to any of the problem-solving exercises as often as you like. It is also recommended that you review the related activities in Practice Project One, p. 17, Practice Project Two, p. 21, and Practice Project Seven, p. 72.

Selected Recordings

We Will Sing! cassette, side 2. Glen Ellyn Children's Chorus.

MY PERFORMANCE PORTFOLIO

O Music, Sweet Music

Name:_____ Date:_____

Self - Evaluation

1. **Describe** your performance of *O Music, Sweet Music.*

    a. Did you perform expressively and sing in tune?

    b. Did you sing smooth legato phrases?

    c. Did you sing all three cadences in tune?

2. **Explain** what you enjoyed most in the rehearsal and performance of this song.

3. **Review** your performance of *O Music, Sweet Music* on audio or video cassette. **Decide** what you like about your performance and what you would like to improve for the next time.

LOTTE MEITNER-GRAF
LONDON

Benjamin Britten (1913-1976)

Orientation

The Sally Gardens

Irish Tune, arr. Benjamin Britten
(1913 – 1976)

Pitch

Vocal Line: Conjunct

Tonality: D♭ major (Begins *do - re - mi*)

Phrase Structure: Each of the two melodically identical verses is made up of four 4-bar phrases

Texture: Unison voices and piano; distinct piano accompaniment; repeated eighth-note chords played in the right hand; melodic motives played in the left hand

Vocal Range:

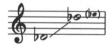

Time

Meter: Duple

Meter Signature: $\frac{2}{2}$

Conduct: In 4

Tempo: Commodo (♩ = 66)

Characteristic Rhythm:

Performance Time: 2′ 35″

Text

Source: Poem by William Butler Yeats (1874-1939) first published in 1908 in *Collected Poems of W.B. Yeats.*

Theme: Unhappy love

Form

Strophic form with two stanzas:
[Intro (4), A (4+4), B (4+4), A (4), interlude (4), A (4+4), B (4), A (4), Code (4)]

Style

Traditional Irish song distinctly set in contemporary style by the celebrated English composer Benjamin Britten; carefully detailed dynamics and staccato articulations help distinguish and contrast a long, legato vocal line with a more rhythmically active accompaniment figure.

Social - Historical

Irish songs often tell stories of life and love; favorite songs are passed down from generation to generation from parent to child, and from friend to friend. Benjamin Britten had a great love of folk songs. He regularly used their melodic themes in both his instrumental and vocal writing.

To Clytie Mundy

THE SALLY GARDENS
Irish Tune

Words by*
W.B. YEATS

Arranged by
BENJAMIN BRITTEN

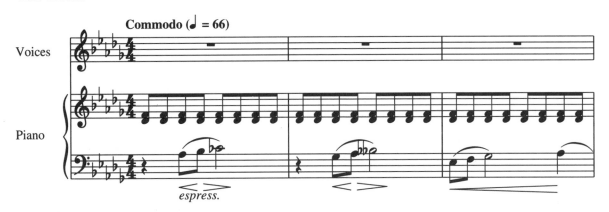

WINTHROP ROGERS EDITION
© Copyright 1958 by Boosey & Co., Ltd. Copyright Renewed. All rights reserved.

*The words of this song are reprinted from "Collected Poems of W.B. Yeats" by permission of Mrs. Yeats.

Rehearsal Guide
The Sally Gardens

Your ability to perform *The Sally Gardens* requires musicianship. In rehearsal, you will have the opportunity to *produce* the song, *practice* the musicianship necessary to meet the musical challenges, and *perform* with skill and understanding.

The musical challenges of performing this song include your ability to:

- **sing** the ascending melodic line from *do* to *do'*;

- **sing** the descending melodic line back to the tonal center D♭ or *do*;

- **sustain** the legato, stepwise motion of the first, second and fourth phrases;

- **prepare** the dynamic and melodic contrast of the third phrase beginning with the interval of a perfect fourth;

- **convey** the meaning of W.B. Yeats' poem.

Producing

1. As your teacher guides you, **listen** for the 4-bar piano introduction and **sing** the first verse of the Irish tune, *The Sally Gardens*.

Practicing

1. On the vowel combination "oo-ah," **vocalize** the melodic outline of the first phrase: *do-so-do'*-so-do. Sustain high *do'* then descend with a decrescendo back down to low *do*. **Vocalize** this exercise in the following keys: D♭, D, E♭, and E.

2. **Listen** to the 4-bar piano interlude, then **sing** the second verse beginning with the text: "In a field by the river…" **Sing** to the end of the piece.

3. **Describe** the third phrase of the second verse: "She bid me take life easy…" **Q:** How do the pitch relationships of the third phrase differ from the other phrases? **Compare** and **contrast** the vocal ranges, intervals, and dynamics of the two types of phrases.

4. Slowly **solfege** the third phrase beginning on m. 32. **Sing** the second verse on solfa to the end.

5. Return to the first verse and **sing** the legato unison line on an *(oo)* vowel, remembering to support the tone on the breath. **Sing** with a rich, warm vocal color.

6. **Compare** the quality of the legato vocal line with the pulsed and rhythmic eighth-note figures in the piano accompaniment. **Describe** how the vocal and piano figures work together to create Britten's interesting arrangement of the Irish tune.

7. **Reading** the 4-bar piano introduction, **clap** the eighth-note rhythm pattern in the right hand of the accompaniment. Using *rhythm syllables,* (see Practice Project Six) **read** the rhythmic figure in the left hand of the accompaniment.

8. **Listen** to Sara, age 12, perform *The Sally Gardens* on the *We Will Sing!* cassette, side 2. As you listen, softly **tap** the eighth-note rhythm pattern you hear in the piano accompaniment.

9. **Write** out the W.B. Yeats poem. Begin the text of each new phrase on a separate line. **Discuss** the meaning and character of the poetry in relation to the dynamic changes that take place throughout the piece.

10. **Answer** these questions regarding the relationship between text and dynamics: **Q:**Why does the final phrase of each verse end softly? **Compare** the final phrase of the first verse with the final phrase of the second verse. **Discuss** Britten's use of dynamics.

11. **Sing** the final phrase of the second verse observing the decrescendo to a *pp* dynamic on the text "foolish."

Performing

1. **Sing** the whole song. Follow your conductor and remember to:

- **sustain** a legato vocal line;

- **begin** each phrase with a preparatory breath;

- **stagger** your breathing throughout each 4-bar phrase to avoid breaking the phrase in two parts;

- **perform** the dynamic changes in relation to W.B. Yeats expressive Irish poem.

Reflecting - Evaluating

You have been learning how to use your singing voice, you have been developing your music reading and counting skills, and you have been studying Benjamin Britten's arrangement of the Irish folksong *The Sally Gardens*. In rehearsal, you *produced* the song with your singing voice, you *practiced* the musicianship required to meet the musical challenges, and you *performed* in class or concert. As you review your performance, complete the following reflections for your journal.

1. **Describe** how you used your voice to perform this song.

2. **Describe** your ability to meet the musical challenges in performing artistically.

3. **Describe** how you could improve your performance.

- As an assessment alternative, you may complete the Self-Evaluation or Concert Critique form to include in your *We Will Sing!* Performance Portfolio.

> To improve your musicianship and to perform artistically, you may return to any of the problem-solving exercises as often as you like. It is also recommended that you review the related activities in Practice Project Five and Practice Project Six, p. 53.

Selected Recordings

Listen to twelve year-old Sara sing Benjamin Britten's arrangement of *The Sally Gardens,* on *We Will Sing* cassette, accompanied by William Buhr.

Another solo performance has been recorded by English tenor Robert Tear.

Folksong Arrangements. Robert Tear, tenor; Philip Ledger, piano. EMI CDM7 69423-2.

You may also enjoy listening to a traditional Irish performance of the folksong *The Sally Gardens,* performed by the Irish group "Clanad."

Clanad in Concert. Shanachie 79030.

M Y   P E R F O R M A N C E   P O R T F O L I O

The Sally Gardens

Name:_____   Date:_____

Self - Evaluation

1. **Describe** your performance of *The Sally Gardens.*

   a. Did you sing expressively and in tune?

   b. Were you able to sustain a legato 4-bar phrase without breaking it into two parts?

2. **Explain** what you enjoyed most in the rehearsal and performance of this Irish tune.

3. **Review** your performance of *The Sally Gardens* on audio or video cassette. **Decide** what you like about your performance and what you would like to improve for the next time.

Orientation

Simple Gifts

Shaker Song, arr. Aaron Copland
(1900 – 1990)

Pitch

Vocal Line: Dance-like, conjunct, mostly step-wise

Tonality: A♭ major (begins *so. - do*)

Phrase Structure: Four 4-bar phrases

Texture: Unison voices with piano accompaniment

Vocal Range:

Time

Meter: Duple

Meter Signature: ²⁄₄

Conduct: In 2

Tempo: (♩ = 72)

Characteristic Rhythm:

Performance Time: 1′ 25″

Text

Source: Shaker hymn

Theme: Simplicity and humility; thanksgiving and joy.

Form

Three-part form: [Intro (2), A (4+4), Interlude (2), B (4+5), Interlude (2), A (4+4), Coda (4)]

Style

The setting is contemporary, "popular" style and tonal; recognized as characteristically American.

Social - Historical

Simple Gifts is selected from Aaron Copland's collection *Old American Songs*. Copland's arrangements of these familiar songs are often performed by solo voice and orchestra. The *Shaker Song* can also be heard in theme and variations in Copland's orchestral suite, *Appalachian Spring,* a ballet he wrote for the beloved American choreographer, Martha Graham.

SIMPLE GIFTS

Arranged by
AARON COPLAND

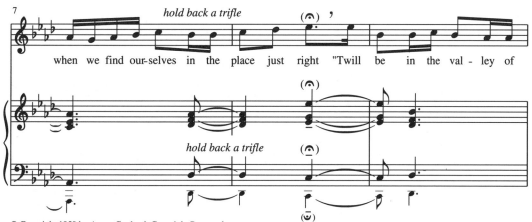

Rehearsal Guide
Simple Gifts 🔲

> Your ability to perform *Simple Gifts* requires musicianship. In rehearsal, you will have the opportunity to *produce* the song, *practice* the musicianship necessary to meet the musical challenges, and *perform* with skill and understanding.

The musical challenges of performing this song include your ability to:

- **sing** the repeated rhythmic and melodic motives that characterize the Shaker Song;

- **support** the contrast in range between the [A] and [B] sections;

- **convey** the meaning of the Shaker hymn text.

Producing

1. **Listen** to the Glen Ellyn Children's Chorus sing Copland's two-part arrangement of *Simple Gifts*. (*We Will Sing!* cassette, side 2) Using your finger, point to the melody line as you follow the unison version in your music textbook. Now you are ready to begin your practice.

Practicing

1. As your teacher guides you, **sing** the entire [A] section of *Simple Gifts* in the following sequence:

   (a) **sing** the first 4-bar phrase (mm. 3-6); then **sing** the second 4-bar phrase (mm. 7-10); repeat the [A] section.

   (b) **identify** where the [B] section begins, then **sing** the entire nine bars. Notice that the [B] section is extended, and that it is longer than the [A] section.

   (c) Sustain the final A♭ cadence for its full rhythmic value.

2. Using the natural rhythm of the words to articulate the rhythm patterns of the music, **chant** the text:

   > *'Tis the gift to be simple,*
   > *'tis the gift to be free... etc.*

3. **Identify** the characteristic rhythm heard most frequently in the [A] section. **Clap** the rhythm pattern, then notate the pattern on the board or on manuscript.

4. Follow the same rehearsal sequence for the [B] section. **Describe** the rhythmic difference between the two sections. Following the score, **chant** and **clap** the rhythm of both sections.

5. Referring to Practice Project Five for a review of score reading, **identify** the key signature of *Simple Gifts*.

6. Using the tonic solfa system of music reading introduced in Practice Project Seven, **identify** *do* in this piece. **Identify** the tonality.

7. **Sing** the first 4-bar phrase of the [A] section with solfa syllables. **Solfege** the second 4-bar phrase of the [A] section.

8. Using the tonic solfa system of music reading, slowly **solfege** the [B] section of *Simple Gifts*. Showing the handsigns introduced in Practice Project Seven, **solfege** and **sign** the [B] section.

9. To challenge your musicianship, return to the [A] section of *Simple Gifts* (m. 3) and solve the following musical problems: **Q:** Where do you hear the very first statement of the opening melodic motive: *so.*-do do-re-mi? Including its statement in the piano introduction, **describe** how many times that same motive is heard in the [A] section?

10. **Solfege** each statement of the motive. Be careful to accurately **read** any variation in the melodic patterns.

11. Where else do you hear the motive: *so.-do do-re-mi?* **Solfege** the final statement of the motive.

12. **Listen** to the piano accompaniment being played without the voice parts. (*We Will Sing* cassette, side 2) **Listen** for the syncopated rhythm and chordal character of the piano parts.

13. **Compare** the music in the accompaniment part to the music in the voice part. **Discuss** the many differences you hear in time and pitch characteristics.

14. **Sing** the [A] section on a sustained (oo) [u] vowel. Support a smooth vocal line in contrast to the rhythmically articulated piano accompaniment. On the higher pitches, **modify** the (oo) [u] vowel toward the (ah) [ɑ] vowel, keeping a smooth, supported, legato line. **Listen** carefully at cadences to support the pure (ah) [ɑ] vowel sound for its full rhythmic value. Repeat the same exercise on the [B] section.

15. **Chant** the Shaker hymn text in a legato style, observing the dynamic changes shown in the score.

16. **Sing** both the [A] and [B] sections with text, supporting a legato line and the expressive dynamic changes.

Performing

1. **Sing** the whole piece. Follow the conductor and remember to:

   • **support** and sustain the legato vocal line;

   • **perform** the dynamic changes, particularly the change in the [B] section;

   • **begin** each phrase with a preparatory breath;

   • **sing** the intervals in tune;

   • **sustain** the ah [ɑ] vowel through the extended cadences.

Reflecting - Evaluating

You have been learning how to use your singing voice, you have been developing your music reading and counting skills, and you have been studying Aaron Copland's arrangement of the Shaker tune *Simple Gifts*. In rehearsal, you *produced* the song with your singing voice, you *practiced* the musicianship required to meet the musical challenges, and you *performed* in class or concert. As you review your performance, complete the following reflections for your journal.

1. **Describe** how you used your voice to perform this song.

2. **Describe** your ability to meet the musical challenges in performing artistically.

3. **Describe** how you could improve your performance.

   • As an assessment alternative, you may complete the Self-Evaluation or Concert Critique form to include in your *We Will Sing!* Performance Portfolio.

To improve your musicianship and to perform artistically, you may return to any of the problem-solving exercises as often as you like. It is also recommended that you review the related activities in Practice Project Seven, p. 72.

Selected Recordings

The piano accompaniment for Aaron Copland's arrangement of the Shaker tune *Simple Gifts* is played by pianist William Buhr on the *We Will Sing!* cassette, side 2.

A solo voice performance with piano may be heard on:

Old American Songs I and II. Roberta Alexander, soprano; Roger Vignoles, piano. Etcetera KTC 1100.

A solo voice performance, accompanied by orchestra may be heard on:

Tribute to Aaron Copland. Bruce Hubbard, baritone; The Orchestra of Saint Luke's, Dennis Russell Davies, conductor. EMI CDC 54282.

Aaron Copland's *Appalachian Spring* is a ballet suite based on variations of the Shaker song "Simple Gifts." Here are two exemplary recordings of this suite:

Appalachian Spring. Boston Symphony Orchestra, Aaron Copland, conductor. RCA Gold Seal 6802-2-RG.

Appalachian Spring: Ballet for Martha. Los Angeles Philharmonic Orchestra, Leonard Bernstein, conductor. Deutsche Grammophon DG 413 324-2GH.

M Y   P E R F O R M A N C E   P O R T F O L I O

Simple Gifts

Name:_____ Date:_____

Self - Evaluation

1. **Describe** your performance of *Simple Gifts*.

    a. Were you able to convey the meaning of the Shaker Song *Simple Gifts*?

    b. Did you achieve a smooth legato line?

    c. Was the [B] section started in tune?

    d. Were the long, sustained cadences of each section sung in tune for their full value?

3. **Compare** and **contrast** your performance of *Simple Gifts* with the Glen Ellyn Children's Chorus recorded version.

4. **Review** your performance of *Simple Gifts* on audio or video cassette. **Decide** what you like about your performance and what you would like to improve for the next time.

Aaron Copland (1900-1990)

Orientation

She's Like the Swallow
Newfoundland folksong
arr: Lori-Anne Dolloff

Pitch

Vocal Line: Mostly conjunct, some chordal skips, especially *mi - la*

Tonality: d minor (Begins: *la. - mi*)

Phrase Structure: Four 4-bar phrases

Texture: Unison voices, piano accompaniment, flute obligato

Vocal Range:

Time

Meter: Triple

Meter Signature: $\frac{3}{4}$

Conduct: In 1 or 3

Tempo: (♩ = 104)

Characteristic Rhythm:

Performance Time: 2' 45''

Text

Source: From Newfoundland, the eastern most Province of Canada; part of a longer song with many verses; each verse has four lines rhyming A - A - B - B.

Theme: Lamenting; telling of a young maid who dies brokenhearted from the difficulties of life; song of love, longing, and regret.

Form

Strophic with three verses and a repeat of the first verse: [A, A′, A′′, A]; the text and accompaniment figure change from verse to verse.

Style

Folksong style; like many folksongs, *She's Like the Swallow* tells a sad story; text is the constantly changing element therefore text is central to the interpretation; the character of the performance should reflect the longing and sadness of the text in relation to the minor tonality.

Social - Historical

One of the most beautiful and well known Newfoundland songs, this arrangement was written especially for classroom choirs. Its has been varied here with the use of triple meter, piano, and flute obligato. Some versions of this song are notated in compound duple meter ($\frac{6}{8}$).

SHE'S LIKE THE SWALLOW

Arranged by
LORI-ANNE DOLLOFF

Rehearsal Guide
She's Like the Swallow

Your ability to perform *She's Like the Swallow* requires musicianship. In rehearsal, you will have the opportunity to *produce* the song, *practice* the musicianship necessary to meet the musical challenges, and *perform* with skill and understanding.

The musical challenges of performing this song include your ability to:

- **interpret** the variation in text from verse to verse;

- **control** the change in dynamics between verses;

- **sustain** the symmetrical phrasing of each verse made up of four 4-bar phrases (16 bars);

- **support** the melodic contour of the 4-bar phrases, rising to high *do* (F) in the middle of each verse, falling back down to *la* (D), at the end of the verse;

- **tune** the altered pitch in each verse (*fa* to *fi*).

Producing

1. **Listen** to the first four measures of piano introduction. As the piano continues to the end of the first verse, **conduct** circular patterns, making one circle to every three beats of music.

2. **Sway** slowly from side to side, or **conduct** in one while your teacher or another student sings the entire first verse.

Practicing

1. As your teacher guides you, **sing** the first verse with your choir (mm. 5-20).

2. **Describe** the length of each phrase. **Q:** How many phrases make up the first verse? The second verse? the third verse? the fourth verse?

3. **Sing** verse two (mm. 25-39).

4. **Compare and contrast** the second verse with the first verse. **Q:** How are these verses the same? How are they different?

5. **Sing** verses three and four.

6. **Describe** how the performer can make each verse sound different.

7. Because the text changes with each verse, and because folksongs like *She's Like the Swallow* tell a story, the form is called *strophic.*

8. **Imagine** another verse to fit this story, and compose a text that would fit this sad, *minor* melody.

9. **Sing** the first verse on the neutral syllable *(ah).* **Sustain** the highest note of the melody, then finish vocalizing the verse. **Identify** by note name the highest pitch in each verse.

10. As the phrases gradually get higher, you must support the tone on the breath. Maintain a good singing posture and begin each phrase with a preparatory breath.

11. **Sing** the first verse using text. Keep a smooth, legato line similar to the one you sang on the sustained (ah) [ɑ] vowel.

12. **Sing** each verse, plus your own verse (optional) with dynamic variation and as much expression as good diction will allow.

Performing

1. **Sing** the whole song uninterrupted. Follow your conductor and remember to:

   • **prepare** each new phrase with a preparatory breath;

   • **sing** a smooth, legato line;

   • **perform** the dynamic changes;

   • **shape** the vowels and articulate the consonants.

Reflecting - Evaluating

You have been learning how to use your singing voice, you have been developing your music reading and counting skills, and you have been studying Lori-Anne Dolloff's arrangement of the Canadian folksong *She's Like the Swallow*. In rehearsal, you *produced* the song with your singing voice, you *practiced* the musicianship required to meet the musical challenges, and you *performed* in class or concert. As you review your performance, complete the following reflections for your journal.

1. **Describe** how you used your voice to perform this song.

2. **Describe** your ability to meet the musical challenges in performing artistically.

3. **Describe** how you could improve your performance.

   • As an assessment alternative, you may complete the Self-Evaluation or Concert Critique form to include in your *We Will Sing!* Performance Portfolio.

To improve your musicianship and to perform artistically, you may return to any of the problem-solving exercises as often as you like. It is also recommended that you review the related activities in Practice Project Seven, p. 78-79.

Selected Recordings

She's Like the Swallow is performed in a Harry Somers' arrangement on:

Spectra. The Elmer Iseler Singers, Elmer Iseler, conductor. Centrediscs CMC 0281.

MY PERFORMANCE PORTFOLIO

She's Like the Swallow

Name:_____ Date:_____

Self - Evaluation

1. **Describe** your performance of *She's Like the Swallow.*

   a. Did you prepare each phrase on the breath?

   b. Did each verse sound slightly different?

   c. Did your own verse fit the music?

   d. Why, or why not?

2. **Review** your performance of *She's Like the Swallow* on audio or video cassette. **Decide** what you like about your performance and what you would like to improve.

Orientation

A Spring Morning
Henry Carey (1687 – 1743)

Pitch

Vocal Line: Lilting, dance-like, mostly conjunct, organized in scale-like passages and sequences

Tonality: E♭ major with modulation to g minor (begins *so - la*)

Phrase Structure: 4-bar phrases throughout

Texture: Unison voices, piano accompaniment

Vocal Range:

Time

Meter: Triple

Meter Signature: ¾ (felt in 1)

Conduct: In 3 or 1

Tempo: Moderato, (about ♩ = 132)

Characteristic Rhythm:

Performance Time: ca. 2′ 10″

Text

Source: A pastoral theme imitating bird calls, piping, singing, and springing; on the subject of nature and love.

Theme: Originally published as "A Pastoral" in 1899, words in this version by H. Lane Wilson, originally published by Boosey & Co. in 1902.

Form

Ternary, A B A da capo: [Intro, A (8+8), A′ (8+4), Interlude, B (8+8), Interlude, A (8+8), Coda]

Style

Pastoral song style, word painting devices to represent bird calls and piping sounds; melismatic passages vocalized on one syllable "ah" contrasting with the predominantly syllabic style; light and dance-like, with the feeling of one pulse per measure.

Social - Historical

Henry Carey was an English composer, poet, playwright, and librettist, who spent most of his career in London writing popular songs like the famous "Sally in our Alley." He rarely used his first name, just "Mr. Carey" appears on his manuscripts.

A SPRING MORNING

A Pastoral

HENRY CAREY
Edited by Doreen Rao

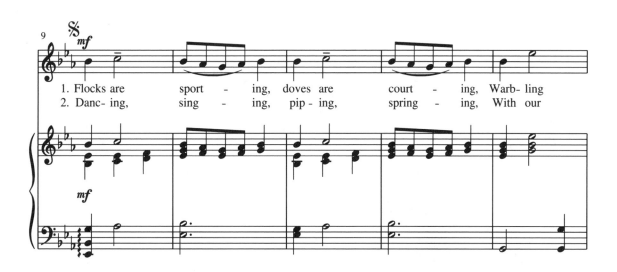

1. Flocks are sport - ing, doves are court - ing, Warb - ling
2. Danc - ing, sing - ing, pip - ing, spring - ing, With our

Rehearsal Guide
A Spring Morning

> Your ability to perform *A Spring Morning* requires musicianship. In rehearsal, you will have the opportunity to *produce* the song, *practice* the musicianship necessary to meet the musical challenges, and *perform* with skill and understanding.

The musical challenges of performing this song include your ability to:

- **feel** the triple meter in 1;

- **articulate** the syncopated rhythm;

- **create** the dance-like movement heard in the repeated melodic patterns (called *sequences*);

- **interpret** the composer's portrayal of springtime sounds and feelings;

- **perform** the contrast between the [A] and [B] sections in tonality, dynamics, and tempo.

Producing

1. To begin your study of "Mr. Carey's" popular English song, **imagine** the sounds and feelings of a spring morning where you live. **Describe** those sounds and feelings as you recall them. **Imitate** the sounds of spring by **chanting, whistling,** or **singing** your own ideas of a spring morning. Your version of a spring morning may be very different from Mr. Carey's version!

Practicing

1. In a light and dance-like character, **clap, conduct,** or **sway** to the music as you **listen** to your teacher play through the [A] section of *A Spring Morning*. **Identify** the musical patterns Mr. Carey used to represent the sounds of a country spring morning.

2. As your teacher guides you, **sing** the [A] section (mm. 9-36) with the text.

3. Composers represent sounds and ideas in music with a compositional technique called *word painting*. **Q:** How does Mr. Carey represent the bird calls and piping sounds in his song *A Spring Morning?* **Q:** What kind of repeated pattern does Mr. Carey use to express his feelings about springtime?

4. As your teacher guides you, **listen** to the first four bars of the piano introduction. To find the pulse, **tap** your toe, or **snap** your fingers in time with the music. The beats are grouped in three, so you already know that the music moves in triple meter.

5. **Listen** again to the first four bars and **describe** the difference between the musical pattern heard in the right hand and the musical pattern heard in the left hand. **Clap** the left hand syncopated rhythm in the first four bars.

6. **Compare** the syncopated rhythm pattern used in the left hand of the piano accompaniment with the rhythm pattern used in the vocal line. Are they the same or different?

7. At m. 9 **chant** the first eight measures of text in rhythm: "Flocks are sporting, doves are courting..." Continuing at bar 25, **chant** the next twelve measures of text in rhythm: "Joy and pleasure..."

8. Refer to Practice Project Five for a review of score reading. **Identify** the key signature of *A Spring Morning.* As you **read** the score, notice that almost every measure of the first eight bars begins on *so* (B♭), except for two bars. **Identify** the two bars that begin on *la* (C).

9. **Solfege** the first note only of mm. 9-16. **Sing** with text the vocal line of these eight measures.

10. **Q:** What pitches seemed most challenging? If you would like to improve your singing, at m. 13, **vocalize** the pitch pattern: *so - do'* (B♭ - E♭). Then **vocalize** the same pitch pattern as it continues into m. 14: *so - do' - la - so.*

11. At m. 25, **solfege** the *first note only* of the next twelve measures. In this section, not all the measures begin on *so* (B♭). With variations along the way, the musical pattern moves downward *so - fa - mi - re,* cadencing on *do* at m. 36. **Vocalize** the descending scale:

12. **Sing** with text the vocal line of mm. 25-36. **Q:** What pitches were most challenging? If you would like to improve your singing at m. 27, **vocalize** the pitch pattern on the open (ah) [ɑ] vowel:

13. **Sing** the [A] section with text, omitting mm. 17-24. Remember to use your best singing posture, prepare your breath for each phrase, and use your singing voice to produce a light and bright choral tone.

14. Beginning at m. 17, **sing** the first note of the next four measures: (*so* - B♭, *fa* - A♭, *mi* - G, *re* - F) then **sing** the entire 4-bar phrase with all the notes in each bar. Repeat this exercise for the second "Ah!" grouping starting at m. 21.

15. **Describe** how Mr. Carey used the compositional technique of *melodic sequence* to represent his feelings about a spring morning.

(A *sequence* is the repetition of a melodic pattern at another pitch.) **Sing** the first melodic sequence from mm. 17-20; **sing** the second melodic sequence from mm. 21-24.

16. **Sing** the entire [A] section beginning at m. 9, ending at m. 36.

17. Following the 4-bar interlude (mm. 37-40), Mr. Carey changes key from E♭ major to g minor. **Sing** the first five notes of a g minor scale:

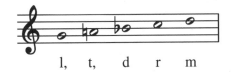

Compare the musical differences between the [A] and [B] sections. **Q:** How can you use your singing voice to convey the contrast between these two sections?

18. At the slow tempo indicated in m. 41, **sing** with text the first 4-bar phrase. At m. 49, **sing** with text this 4-bar phrase. **Compare** and **contrast** these two phrases.

19. Return to m. 45. Slowly **solfege** mm. 45-48 and mm. 53-56. The challenges of these descending intervals, in mm. 53 and 54 especially, will require careful practice. Use this solfege exercise to master these musical intervals.

20. **Sing** the entire g minor [B] section with text.

Performing

1. **Sing** the whole song. Follow your conductor and remember to:

   • **keep** a good singing posture;

   • **prepare** each new phrase with a preparatory breath;

   • **keep** the vowels pure and bright in color;

   • **articulate** the syncopated rhythms with exact diction;

   • **differentiate** tone color between the major and minor sections.

Reflecting - Evaluating

You have been learning how to use your singing voice, you have been developing your music reading and counting skills, and you have been studying Henry Carey's *A Spring Morning*. In rehearsal, you *produced* the song with your singing voice, you *practiced* the musicianship required to meet the musical challenges, and you *performed* in class or concert. As you review your performance, complete the following reflections for your journal.

1. **Describe** how you used your voice to perform this song.

2. **Describe** your ability to meet the musical challenges in performing artistically.

3. **Describe** how you could improve your performance.

   • As an assessment alternative, you may complete the Self-Evaluation or Concert Critique form to include in your *We Will Sing!* Performance Portfolio.

To improve your musicianship and to perform artistically, you may return to any of the problem-solving exercises as often as you like. It is also recommended that you review the related activities in Practice Projects One through Seven.

M Y   P E R F O R M A N C E   P O R T F O L I O

A Spring Morning

Name:_____ Date:_____

Self - Evaluation

1. **Describe** your performance of *A Spring Morning*.

   a. Did you sing expressively and in tune?

   b. Were you able to convey the contrasting character between the [A] and [B] sections?

   3. Did you sing the melodic "Ah!" sequence in a legato and dance-like manner?

2. **Describe** your intonation in the G minor section. How could you improve your intonation for future performances?

3. **Describe** your ability to convey the sounds and feelings of a spring morning.

4. How are "Mr. Carey's" musical sounds different than your own versions of the sounds and feelings of spring you produced at the beginning of your rehearsal?

7. **Review** your performance of *A Spring Morning* on audio or video cassette. **Decide** what you like about your performance and what you would like to improve.

Orientation

Good Night

Dmitri Kabalevsky (1904 – 1987)

Pitch

Vocal Line: Descending 2-bar motive followed by an ascending sequence climaxing at the octave.

Tonality: d minor (begins on *mi*)

Phrase Structure: 4-bar phrases

Texture: Unison voices (optional two-part), piano

Vocal Range:

Time

Meter: Duple

Meter Signature: $\frac{2}{4}$

Conduct: In 2

Tempo: Larghetto, (ca. ♩ = 66)

Characteristic Rhythm:

$\frac{2}{4}$

Performance Time: ca. 1′ 45″

Text

Source: Taught to Doreen Rao by Dmitri Kabalevsky in 1966 as a symbol of their friendship.

Theme: Lullaby assuring a child that night is coming and it is time to sleep; translated into English from Russian.

Pronunciation:

Russian Word	IPA Symbol	Translation
Spakoinyi	[spɑkoinyi]	Good
notsi	[nɔtʃi]	Night

Form

Binary A B A B: [Intro (4), A (4+4), B (4+8), Interlude (4), A (4+4), B (4+8), Coda (5)]

Style

In the character of a Russian lullaby, a swaying, rocking, legato line imaging the scene of a mother rocking her child; simple and in hushed tones.

Social - Historical

Composer Dmitri Kabalevsky is best known for his instrumental compositions, especially his piano works for students. But his fame in Russia centers around his vocal writing and philosophy of music education. Doreen Rao's arrangement for young choirs was first performed at the American Orff Schulwerk National Conference in Chicago in November 1987 by the Glen Ellyn Children's Chorus. The arrangement is dedicated to Mr. Kabalevsky's memory for his lifelong commitment to the music education of children throughout the world.

GOOD NIGHT

DMITRI KABALEVSKY
Arranged by Doreen Rao

Rehearsal Guide

Good Night

Your ability to perform *Good Night* requires musicianship. In rehearsal, you will have the opportunity to *produce* the song, *practice* the musicianship necessary to meet the musical challenges, and *perform* with skill and understanding.

The musical challenges of performing this song include your ability to:

- **feel** the slow rocking motion of duple meter;

- **tune** the minor tonality;

- **perform** the second section in two parts singing expressively and in tune;

- **sing** the optional Russian text: "Spakoinyi notši" (*Good night*).

Producing

1. **Moving** gently from side to side, close your eyes and show how you might rock a baby to sleep.

2. **Listen** to the Glen Ellyn Children's Chorus sing *Good Night* (*We Will Sing!* cassette, side 2). Following the score, **describe** how the musical qualities of tonality, tempo, and dynamics characterize this song as a lullaby.

Practicing

1. Referring to Practice Project Seven (Minor Tonality) **identify** the tonality and the general direction of the melodic line.

2. **Vocalize** the descending minor scale below. Prepare the exercise with a good breath and make a decrescendo as the line descends.

m   r   d   t,   l,

3. **Vocalize** this solfa pattern making a decrescendo as you descend.

l - m - l,

4. On a hissing "ts" sound, practice the breathing exercise on this short rhythm pattern:

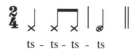

ts - ts - ts - ts

5. As your teacher guides you, **listen** to the 4-bar piano introduction, and **sing** through the first four measures of the melody using text.

6. **Identify** the next place you find the same melody. **Sing** from m. 29 to m. 32. **Q:** Is there another statement of the same melody? **Sing** it using text.

7. At m. 9, **solfege** the ascending melodic sequence through m. 12. Add the missing solfa syllables. **Q:** Did you notice how the 4-bar melodic sequence is based on the ascending scale *ti - do - re - mi*?

t, __ __ d __ __ r __ __ m

Continuing at m. 13, **solfege** the descending line *la - so - mi*. Then **sing** the complete 4-bar phrase, mm. 13-16, using text.

8. Another melodic sequence begins at m. 18 with the descending pattern: *la - so - fa - mi - la.*. Using handsigns (see Practice Project Seven, p. 71), **solfege** the first statement at mm. 18-19. **Q:** How is the next phrase at mm.

20-21 different from mm. 18-19? Slowly **solfege** the entire sequence holding the first note of each of the three short phrases.

9. **Sing** the entire [B] section with text starting at m. 13 through m. 26.

10. **Sing** the Voice I part in unison with text from mm. 29-50.

11. **Sing** the whole song again in unison until you feel very secure and in control of the music. When you feel ready, and when your teacher agrees that your unison singing is secure and expressive, you may begin rehearsing the two-part section from mm. 29-50.

12. As you begin to study the Voice II part, **compare** and **contrast** the Voice II material with the Voice I material. **Q:**How is it the same? How is it different?

13. The whole class can learn to sing the Voice II material, then you and your teacher can **decide** how to divide the group for part singing.

14. *Good Night* may be performed in unison or in two-parts. Whichever way your class performs Mr. Kabalevsky's song, remember to **sing** in the "lullaby style." With good posture and breath preparation, **control** the soft dynamic singing, and **perform** the dynamic changes indicated throughout the score. Dynamics are very important to expressive performance.

Performing

1. **Sing** the whole song from beginning to end without interruption. Remember to:

   • **sing** in the Russian "lullaby style";

   • **support** the legato line and the piano dynamics;

   • **shape** the crescendi and decrescendi;

   • **listen** to the sustained cadence points and **tune** by singing soft open vowels.

Reflecting - Evaluating

You have been learning how to use your singing voice, you have been developing your music reading and counting skills, and you have been studying Dmitri Kabalevsky's *Good Night*. In rehearsal, you *produced* the song with your singing voice, you *practiced* the musicianship required to meet the musical challenges, and you *performed* in class or concert. As you review your performance, complete the following reflections for your journal.

1. **Describe** how you used your voice to perform this song.

2. **Describe** your ability to meet the musical challenges in performing artistically.

3. **Describe** how you could improve your performance.

   • As an assessment alternative, you may complete the Self-Evaluation or Concert Critique form to include in your *We Will Sing!* Performance Portfolio.

To improve your musicianship and to perform artistically, you may return to any of the problem-solving exercises as often as you like. It is also recommended that you review the related activities in Practice Project Six, p. 61-62 and Practice Project Seven, p. 78.

Selected Recordings

We Will Sing! cassette, side 2. Glen Ellyn Children's Chorus.

You may enjoy listening to other examples of Russian Folk Music. *Folk Music of the U.S.S.R.* is an excellent collection of choral and instrumental folk music from the many different regions of the former Soviet Union.

Folk Music of the U.S.S.R. Folkways Records FE 4535 C/D.

Performance Projects: Program One

M Y   P E R F O R M A N C E   P O R T F O L I O

Good Night

Name:_____ Date:_____

Self - Evaluation

1. **Describe** your performance of *Good Night*.

    a. Did you sing expressively and in tune?

    b. Were you able to convey the Russian "lullaby style" at a slow tempo with contrasting dynamics?

    c. Were the d minor cadences sustained in tune for their entire value?

    d. Did you support the descending vocal lines with good singing posture and breath control?

    e. If you sang in two parts in the second section, were you able to maintain good intonation and clear diction?

2. **Review** your performance of *Good Night* on audio or video casette. **Decide** what you like about your performance and what you would like to improve.

PERFORMANCE PROJECTS

Program Two

Orientation

Jubilate Deo
Michael Praetorius (1571-1621)

Pitch

Vocal Line: Ascending stepwise motion to the major third: *do' - re' - mi'*; descending to the final statement one octave lower: *do - so - so - do*.

Tonality: C major (Begins on *do'*)

Phrase Structure: Three statements of 2-bar phrases

Texture: Unison song, unaccompanied; optional canon in two, three, or four parts (*polyphony*)

Vocal Range:

Time

Meter: Duple

Meter Signature: $\frac{2}{2}$

Conduct: In 2

Tempo: Adagio ($\downarrow$ = ca. 69)

Characteristic Rhythm: Varied

Performance Time: ad lib.

Text

Source: Latin text based on Psalm 65: "Rejoice in the Lord, Alleluia"

Theme: Praise and rejoicing

Pronunciation:

Latin Word	IPA Symbol	Translation
Jubilate	[j u b i L a t e]	Rejoice!
Deo	[d e o]	God
Alleluia	[a L e L u j a]	Alleluia

Form

Canon in two, three, or four parts, repeated ad lib.

Style

Polyphonic (*canonic:* each voice sings the same melody at a different time); Renaissance motet developed from a conjunct repeated melody, ending with an almost harmonic bass-like figure; linear and legato. Style requires sensitivity to the shape of line, pure tone, and distinction of moving parts.

Social - Historical

Michael Praetorius was a German composer who lived during the Renaissance period. During his childhood, Praetorius spent many years singing soprano in a boychoir. In the late 16th century, he wrote the short *Jubilate Deo* as part of a longer motet. In Renaissance music, tempo is taken from the natural flow of text and human pulse. Dynamic contrasts are achieved by the layering and adding of voices. Musical interest is achieved by the character of the melodic lines as they move in imitative style (*polyphony*) to reflect the text meaning.

JUBILATE DEO

Psalm 65

MICHAEL PRAETORIUS
Arranged by Doreen Rao

Rehearsal Guide

Jubilate Deo 🔘

> Your ability to perform *Jubilate Deo* requires musicianship. In rehearsal, you will have the opportunity to *produce* the song, *practice* the musicianship necessary to meet the musical challenges, and *perform* with skill and understanding.

The musical challenges of performing this song include your ability to:

- **support** the ascending melody to the major third (*mi* - E);

- **distinguish** between the three contrasting phrases;

- **prepare** the wide range of pitches from middle C to high E;

- **perform** in canon.

Producing

1. Using your best singing posture, **sing** *Jubilate Deo*. Your teacher will guide you as you sing in unison with your choir.

Practicing

1. **Speak** the Latin text: "Ju-bi-la-te De-o. Al-le-lu-ia." (See the pronunciation guide in the *Jubilate Deo* Orientation.)

2. **Describe** the sound of the Latin text: **Q:** Is it bright? dark? **Read** the text translation in the Orientation. How does the sound of the Latin text reflect the text meaning of praise and rejoicing?

3. **Sing** the first 2-bar phrase with text. **Listen** for the ascending melody to the major third (*mi'* - E). Repeat the first phrase on the neutral syllable "ah" [*a*] holding the highest note until it sounds in tune.

4. **Sing** the second 2-bar phrase with text. Keep the (ah) [*a*] vowel of "Jubi<u>la</u>te" pure and supported.

5. **Sing** the third 2-bar phrase on the text "Alleluia." **Sing** this section more rhythmically, especially on the repeated quarter note *so* (G).

6. Referring back to Practice Project Seven for a review of tonic solfa, slowly **solfege** and **sign** each phrase. This exercise will give you a sense of the melodic movement.

7. **Sing** the entire unison melody with text in the spirit of rejoicing. Keep the vowels pure and bright. For a review of vocal phonetics, refer to Practice Project Four. **Listen** for the differences between the three contrasting phrases.

8. When you feel ready, and your conductor agrees that your unison singing is secure, you may begin rehearsing in canon. Singing in canon creates what is called *polyphony*.

9. Experiment by standing in various places in the room and filling the room with sound. During the Renaissance period (1450-1600), this motet would have been performed in a large cathedral acoustic.

Performing

1. **Sing** the whole piece. Follow the conductor and remember to:

- **start** each new phrase with a preparatory breath;

- **sing** pure and bright vowels;

- **sing** accurately and in tune;

- **sing** the final phrase with rhythmic definition.

Reflecting - Evaluating

You have been learning how to use your singing voice, you have been developing your music reading and counting skills, and you have been studying Michael Praetorius' *Jubilate Deo*. In rehearsal, you *produced* the song with your singing voice, you *practiced* the musicianship required to meet the musical challenges, and you *performed* in class or concert. As you review your performance, complete the following reflections for your journal.

1. **Describe** how you used your voice to perform this song.

2. **Describe** your ability to meet the musical challenges in performing artistically.

3. **Describe** how you could improve your performance.

   • As an assessment alternative, you may complete the Self-Evaluation or Concert Critique form to include in your *We Will Sing!* Performance Portfolio.

To improve your musicianship and to perform artistically, you may return to any of the problem-solving exercises as often as you like. It is also recommended that you review the related activities in Practice Project Four, p. 34 and p. 37, and Practice Project Seven, p. 69-72.

Selected Recordings

We Will Sing! cassette, side 2. Glen Ellyn Children's Chorus.

You may enjoy listening to another example of a short Praetorius motet, *Psallite* on:

Sweet was the Song. The Vancouver Chamber Choir, Jon Washburn, conductor. Marquis ERAD 107.

M Y   P E R F O R M A N C E   P O R T F O L I O

Jubilate Deo

Name:_____ Date:_____

Self - Evaluation

1.**Describe** your performance of *Jubilate Deo*.

    a. Did you communicate expressively and sing in tune?

    b. Did you sing bright and pure vowels?

    c. Did you convey the meaning of praise and rejoicing?

    d. **Explain** what you enjoyed most about your performance of this song.

2. **Review** your performance of *Jubilate Deo* on audio or video cassette. **Decide** what you like about your performance and what you would like to improve.

Orientation

The Path to the Moon
Eric H. Thiman (1900 – 1975)

Pitch

Vocal Line: Conjunct motion; skips in octaves, fourths, and thirds; built on melodic sequence.

Tonality: A♭ major (Begins *so - so'*)

Phrase Structure: 4-bar phrases

Texture: Unison voices with piano accompaniment

Vocal Range:

Time

Meter: Compound duple

Meter Signature: ⁶⁄₈

Conduct: In 2

Tempo: Andantino (♩. = ca. 48)

Characteristic Rhythm:

⁶⁄₈ ♩ 𝄽 ♪ ♩ 𝄽

Performance Time: 2′ 40″

Text

Source: Written by Madeline C. Thomas

Theme: Dream-like, poetic fantasy

Form

Through-composed [Intro (4), A (8), B (4), Interlude (4), A (8), Interlude (2), A′ (2), B (4), Coda (4)]

Style

Contemporary English song written in Romantic style with long, melodic lines, rich harmonies, and dynamic contrasts to convey the poetic fantasy of sailing to the moon.

Social - Historical

English composer Eric Thiman was a music teacher and well-known organist who wrote music for amateur musicians. His solo songs are performed frequently in North America by professional singers and student musicians alike. Mr. Thiman taught on the Faculty of Music at London University. His music is characterized by beautiful melodies, uncomplicated harmonies, and short forms.

THE PATH TO THE MOON

MADELINE C. THOMAS

ERIC H. THIMAN

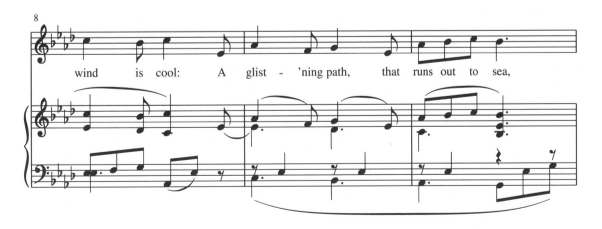

Rehearsal Guide
The Path to the Moon

Your ability to perform *The Path to the Moon* requires musicianship. In rehearsal, you will have the opportunity to *produce* the song, *practice* the musicianship necessary to meet the musical challenges, and *perform* with skill and understanding.

The musical challenges of performing this song include your ability to:

- **feel** the lilting, ⁶⁄₈ movement;

- **support** the octave interval *so - so'* (E♭ - E♭) followed by a pattern of descending thirds;

- **contrast** the changing dynamics, particularly the subito piano at m. 33 to the final cadence;

- **sustain** the dotted rhythms in the compound meter.

Producing

1. **Swaying** slowly from side to side, **clap** three beats to each sway or six beats to every two sways. **Chant** Madeline Thomas' poem to the feeling of the sway. **Sustain** the underlined words a little longer than the other words:

   I <u>long</u> to <u>sail</u> the <u>path</u> to the <u>moon</u>
   On a <u>deep</u> blue night
   when the <u>wind</u> is <u>cool;</u>
   A <u>glistening</u> <u>path</u> that runs out to <u>sea,</u>
   Silver the <u>sails</u> to <u>carry</u> me,
   to <u>carry</u> me over the <u>sea.</u>

   So will I <u>sail</u> on a <u>starry</u> <u>night</u>
   On the path to the <u>Moon,</u>
   a <u>seabirds</u> <u>flight;</u>
   Skimming the <u>waves</u>
   where the <u>fishes</u> <u>play,</u>
   Traveling <u>on</u> for many a <u>day;</u>

   Silver the <u>sails</u> to <u>carry</u> me,
   to <u>carry</u> me over the <u>sea.</u>

Practicing

1. **Listen** to the Glen Ellyn Children's Chorus sing *The Path to the Moon* (*We Will Sing!* cassette, side 2). Following your score, **identify** the compound meter and determine how many times you hear the melodic pattern notated here:

   s   m   f   r   m   d   r

2. Slowly **swaying** from side to side, **sing** the first two bars (mm. 5-6) using tonic solfa. **Identify** the next place you find the same melodic pattern.

3. **Sing** the return of this melodic pattern (mm. 21-22). **Identify** the next place you find the same melodic pattern.

4. **Sing** the final statement of this melody (mm. 31-32). **Q:** Did you notice that each time this melody is stated, the words change?

5. Return to the beginning of the piece and look at the simple 4-bar refrain that begins with the text "to carry…" (mm. 13-16). **Sing** the refrain with text being careful to avoid the "r" sound on the first syllable of the word "carry." Sustain the [æ] vowel as you would hear it sounded in the English word "ask." **Identify** the next place you find the same 4-bar refrain.

6. **Sing** the final 4-bar refrain starting at m. 33. **Q:** Did you notice the rhythmic variation of the final statement at m. 36?

7. **Speak** the rhythm at m. 33 with text. **Count** the rhythm on the numbers "<u>1</u> - 2 - <u>3</u> - 4 - <u>5</u> - 6" stressing 1, 3, and 5. **Sing** mm. 36-37. This rhythmic alteration is called *hemiola,* a term applied to time values that are in the relationship 3:2. The feeling of triple or three can be

felt in the piano accompaniment. This is heard against the feeling of duple or two in the voice part.

8. **Q:** Why to you think the composer used *hemiola* in his last statement of the refrain "to carry me over the sea?"

9. **Sing** the first section with text (mm. 5-16). **Q:** How many bars is the first interlude? (mm. 17-20) **Sing** the second section with text (mm. 21-28). **Q:** How many bars is the second interlude? **Sing** the third section with text (mm. 31-37). **Q:** How many bars is the *coda*? (A *coda* is a final section of music added to make a piece sound final.) In *The Path to the Moon,* the coda begins at m. 27 with the new material in the piano accompaniment.

Performing

1. **Sing** the whole song from start to finish without stopping (if you can!). Follow the conductor and remember to:

   • **prepare** each new phrase with a breath;

   • **sustain** the legato § feel and "stretch" the quarter-note rhythms to keep the phrase moving forward;

   • **sing** the important dynamic contrasts indicated in each section, especially the subito piano dynamic of the final refrain.

Reflecting - Evaluating

You have been learning how to use your singing voice, you have been developing your music reading and counting skills, and you have been studying Eric Thiman's *The Path to the Moon.* In rehearsal, you *produced* the song with your singing voice, you *practiced* the musicianship required to meet the musical challenges, and you *performed* in class or concert. As you review your performance, complete the following reflections for your journal.

1. **Describe** how you used your voice to perform this song.

2. **Describe** your ability to meet the musical challenges in performing artistically.

3. **Describe** how you could improve your performance.

   • As an assessment alternative, you may complete the Self-Evaluation or Concert Critique form to include in your *We Will Sing!* Performance Portfolio.

> To improve your musicianship and to perform artistically, you may return to any of the problem-solving exercises as often as you like. It is also recommended that you review the related activities in Practice Project Six, p. 54 and p. 60.

Selected Recordings

We Will Sing! cassette, side 2. Glen Ellyn Children's Chorus.

M Y P E R F O R M A N C E P O R T F O L I O

The Path to the Moon

Name:_____ Date:_____

Self - Evaluation

1. **Describe** your performance of *The Path to the Moon*.

    a. Did you sing expressively and in tune?

    b. Were you able to support a legato § rhythm without "letting go" of the sustained quarter notes?

2. **Explain** what you enjoyed most in the rehearsal and performance of this popular English song by Eric Thiman.

3. **Review** your performance of *The Path to the Moon* on audio or video cassette. **Decide** what you like about your performance and what you would like to improve.

Orientation

I Know Where I'm Goin'
Traditional Irish Country Song
arr. Herbert Hughes

Pitch

Vocal Line: Conjunct, ascending stepwise

Tonality: G Major (Begins on *do*)

Phrase Structure: 4-bar phrases

Texture: Unison voices and piano accompaniment

Vocal Range:

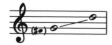

Time

Meter: Duple

Meter Signature: $\frac{2}{4}$

Conduct: In 2

Tempo: Larghetto (♩ = ca. 63)

Characteristic Rhythm:

Performance Time: ca. 2′

Text

Source: Irish Country Song

Theme: On the popular subject of romance and marriage

Form

Strophic. Five verses are varied by changing text and dynamics. Last verse contrast is created by accompaniment figure.

Style

Popular Irish songs like this one are performed in a melodic, playful, and story-like manner. Attention to the text is the key to interpretation.

Social - Historical

This song was collected and arranged by Herbert Hughes in his 1909 volume "Irish Country Songs" published by Boosey & Hawkes. Traditional Irish songs often vary from singer to singer. Likewise, there are many different arrangements of this simple Irish ballad.

I KNOW WHERE I'M GOIN'

from *Irish Country Songs* of
HERBERT HUGHES
Adapted and arranged by
Doreen Rao

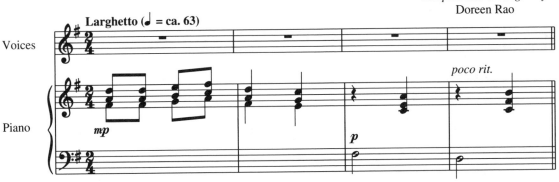

1. I know where I'm go - in', And I know who's go - in' with me,
2. I have stockings of silk, Shoes of fine green lea - ther,

I know who I love, But the dear knows* who I'll mar - ry!
Combs to buck-le my hair, And a ring for ev - 'ry fin - ger.

*"Dear knows" the Ulster equivalent of "Goodness knows".

Rehearsal Guide

I Know Where I'm Goin'

Your ability to perform *I Know Where I'm Goin'* requires musicianship. In rehearsal, you will have the opportunity to *produce* the song, *practice* the musicianship necessary to meet the musical challenges, and *perform* with skill and understanding.

The musical challenges of performing this song include your ability to:

- **support** legato phrases with clear diction;

- **prepare** in-tune pitches beginning on *do* (G) and *so* (D);

- **contrast** changing dynamics throughout;

- **perform** a dramatic, story-telling interpretation.

Producing

1. **Read** the text of all five verses to determine the story. **Decide** how you will interpret the five verse story in a musical, expressive performance. Pay close attention to the important musical changes in the final verse.

Practicing

1. **Listen** to your teacher play the 4-bar piano introduction.

2. Find *do* and **identify** the tonality of the song.

3. **Sing** verse one with text. **Hold** (⌢) the highest note, then continue to the end of verse one. **Solfege** and **sign** the G major ascending scale from *do* (G) to *so* (D).

4. **Solfege** and **sign** the descending interval of a perfect 5th in mm. 9-10.

5. **Solfege** and **sign** *so - do - ti.* .

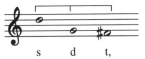

6. **Sing** verse two with text. **Listen** for the descending perfect 5th *so - do* (D - G) and the descending half-step *do - ti.* (G - F♯). Notice the change in rhythmic notation that mirrors the natural rhythm of the text.

7. **Identify** the dynamic marking at m. 15. **Describe** how you would like to interpret verses three and four.

8. **Sing** verse five with text. **Compare** verse five with verse one. **Describe** how the first and last verses contrast.

9. **Prepare** the fermata at m. 30 with a full breath. Stagger your breathing while holding the fermata on *do* (G). *(Staggered breathing requires that each singer breathe at a different time.)*

10. **Watch** the conductor carefully to determine how fast you should sing the *accelerando* in mm. 31-32.

Performing

1. **Sing** all five verses without stopping. Follow your conductor and remember to:

   • **sing** smooth, legato phrases;

   • **prepare** each phrase with a full breath;

   • **sing** in tune at all times;

   • **observe** dynamic markings and tempo changes;

   • **interpret** each verse differently, using text, dynamics, and tempo variation to create the story-telling drama characteristic of Irish folksongs.

Reflecting - Evaluating

You have been learning how to use your singing voice, you have been developing your music reading and counting skills, and you have been studying Herbert Hughes' arrangement of the Irish folksong *I Know Where I'm Goin'*. In rehearsal, you *produced* the song with your singing voice, you *practiced* the musicianship required to meet the musical challenges, and you *performed* in class or concert. As you review your performance, complete the following reflections for your journal.

1. **Describe** how you used your voice to perform this song.

2. **Describe** your ability to meet the musical challenges in performing artistically.

3. **Describe** how you could improve your performance.

   • As an assessment alternative, you may complete the Self-Evaluation or Concert Critique form to include in your *We Will Sing!* Performance Portfolio.

To improve your musicianship and to perform artistically, you may return to any of the problem-solving exercises as often as you like. It is also recommended that you review the related activities in Practice Project Six, p. 51.

Selected Recordings

You may enjoy listening to a traditional performance of *I Know Where I'm Goin'*, accompanied by harp on:

Irish Harp Songs. Performed by Emily Mitchell. RCA Victor 7860-2.

M Y   P E R F O R M A N C E   P O R T F O L I O

I Know Where I'm Goin'

Name:_____ Date:_____

Self - Evaluation

1. **Describe** your performance of *I Know Where I'm Goin'*.

   a. Did you perform expressively and sing in tune?

   b. How did your interpretation create a story?

   c. **Describe** the tone color you produced in relation to the Irish folk song style.

2. **Explain** what you enjoyed most in the rehearsal and performance of this Irish song.

3. **Review** your performance of *I Know Where I'm Goin'* on audio or video cassette. **Decide** what you like about your performance and what you would like to improve.

Orientation

Oliver Cromwell
Rhyme song from Suffolk
arr. Benjamin Britten (1913 – 1976)

Pitch

Vocal Line: Descending disjunct melodic motive outlines tonic chord

Tonality: E♭ major (Begins on *do'*)

Phrase Structure: 4-bar phrases sometimes felt in 2 + 2

Texture: Unison voices with piano accompaniment

Vocal Range:

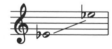

Time

Meter: duple/compound duple

Meter Signature: $\frac{2}{4}$ ($\frac{6}{8}$)

Conduct: In 2

Tempo: Vivace ($\quarternote$ = 160)

Characteristic Rhythm:

Performance Time: 45″

Text

Source: Nursery rhyme from Suffolk

Theme: Political joke (satire) about Oliver Cromwell, a Puritan leader disliked by the people of England.

Form

Strophic; 4-bar melody repeated twice in each verse. [Intro (8), A (4+4), Interlude (2), A′ (4+4), Interlude (4), A″ (4+4), Interlude (2), A‴ (4+4)]

Style

English, contemporary (20th century); light-hearted, joking, speech-like, and rhythmic.

Social - Historical

Oliver Cromwell was an English ruler from 1653 – 1658. He lived from 1599 – 1658, and became ruler after he and his Puritan forces defeated the Royalists in the Civil War of the 1640's. His forces disposed of King Charles I. Oliver Cromwell was strict and cruel, disliked by the people of England for his puritanical rule. Nursery rhymes were often a way people recorded historical events and expressed political opinions in a light-hearted manner. Hence, this musical joke that he gave an old woman "a drop" that made her go "hippety hop" "Heehaw!" Benjamin Britten arranged the Suffolk nursery rhyme in a way that captures the humor of the story and the military, puritan character of Oliver Cromwell.

To Christopher Mayer

OLIVER CROMWELL

Nursery Rhyme from Suffolk

Arranged by
BENJAMIN BRITTEN

N. B. *Where a large choir is used it is recommended that the alternate phrases be sung by full chorus and semi-chorus*

Hee - haw— hip - pe - ty hop.

The sad - dle and bri - dle, they lie on the shelf,

Hee - haw— lie on the shelf, if you want a - ny more you can

sing it your-self, Hee - haw— sing it your-self.

Rehearsal Guide

Oliver Cromwell

> Your ability to perform *Oliver Cromwell* requires musicianship. In rehearsal, you will have the opportunity to *produce* the song, *practice* the musicianship necessary to meet the musical challenges, and *perform* with skill and understanding.

The musical challenges of performing this song include your ability to:

- **support** the descending E♭ major chordal melody;

- **articulate** the speech-like rhythmic motive with exact, clear diction;

- **sing** the varied dynamic requirements with breath support and vocal control;

- **perform** the humorous and light-hearted text with expressive interpretation.

Producing

1. **Read** the story of *Oliver Cromwell* and **discuss** the nature of this historical rhyme.

   Oliver Cromwell lay buried and dead,
   Hee-haw buried and dead,
   There grew an old apple tree over his head,
   Hee-haw over his head.

   The apples were ripe and ready to fall;
   Hee-haw ready to fall;
   there came an old woman to gather them all,
   Hee-haw gather them all.

   Oliver rose and gave her a drop,
   Hee-haw gave her a drop,
   which made the old woman go hippety hop,
   Hee-haw hippety hop.

   The saddle and bridle, they lie on the shelf,
   Hee-haw lie on the shelf,
   if you want any more you can sing it yourself
   Hee-haw sing it yourself.

Practicing

1. **Chant** the text rhythmically. **Listen** for the contrast between the short, syllabic eighth-note rhythms and the sustained, dotted quarter-note rhythms of the text "Hee-haw."

2. **Solfege** the descending E♭ major chord that shapes the *Oliver Cromwell* melody:

   d'   s   m   d

3. **Sing** the first verse of *Oliver Cromwell* using text (mm. 9-16).

4. **Listen** to the Glen Ellyn Children's Chorus recording of this song (*We Will Sing!* cassette, side 2). **Describe** how the chorus interpreted the song. (The Selected Recordings list in this Rehearsal Guide suggests other performances of *Oliver Cromwell*.) If you listen to other recordings, you can compare interpretations.

5. **Identify** the dynamics used in the written score and **decide** how Britten used dynamics to create interest in his arrangement.

6. **Sing** the verse that begins at a "*p*" dynamic and ends with a "*pp*" dynamic. **Describe** the dramatic effect created by these dynamics.

7. **Listen** to a recorded performance of Britten's arrangement of *Oliver Cromwell* and follow the piano accompaniment. **Q:** How does Britten use the piano to develop and enhance his arrangement?

8. **Sing** only the *unaccompanied* material throughout the song.

9. **Sing** only the *accompanied* material throughout the song.

10. **Sing** all four verses **listening** for the changing accompaniment.

Performing

1. **Sing** the whole song from beginning to end. Follow the conductor and remember to:

   • **prepare** each phrase with a breath;

   • **control** the dynamic changes;

   • **sing** exact rhythms with clear vocal diction;

   • **perform** all four verses in tempo being careful in the final verse not to slow down (*senza rit.*);

   • **interpret** the drama and meaning of the Suffolk rhyme in your performance.

Reflecting - Evaluating

You have been learning how to use your singing voice, you have been developing your music reading and counting skills, and you have been studying Benjamin Britten's arrangement of *Oliver Cromwell*. In rehearsal, you *produced* the song with your singing voice, you *practiced* the musicianship required to meet the musical challenges, and you *performed* in class or concert. As you review your performance, complete the following reflections for your journal.

1. **Describe** how you used your voice to perform this song.

2. **Describe** your ability to meet the musical challenges in performing artistically.

3. **Describe** how you could improve your performance.

   • As an assessment alternative, you may complete the Self-Evaluation or Concert Critique form to include in your *We Will Sing!* Performance Portfolio.

To improve your musicianship and to perform artistically, you may return to any of the problem-solving exercises as often as you like. It is also recommended that you review the related activities in Practice Project Six, p. 63.

Selected Recordings

We Will Sing! cassette, side 2. Glen Ellyn Children's Chorus.

A solo performance of Benjamin Britten's arrangement of *Oliver Cromwell* has been recorded by tenor Robert Tear on:

Folksong Arrangements. Robert Tear, tenor; Philip Ledger, piano. EMI CDM7 69423-2.

M Y   P E R F O R M A N C E   P O R T F O L I O

Oliver Cromwell

Name:_____ Date:_____

Self - Evaluation

1. **Describe** your performance of *Oliver Cromwell.*

   a. Did your interpretation of *Oliver Cromwell* capture the satirical, humorous nature of the rhyme?

   b. How did you create dramatic interest in the final verse?

   c. Were the rhythms and pitches exact?

2. **Explain** what you enjoyed most in the rehearsal and performance of this song.

3. **Review** your performance of *Oliver Cromwell* on audio or video cassette. **Decide** what you like about your performance and what you would like to improve.

Orientation

Bist du bei mir
J.S. Bach (1685 – 1750)

Pitch

Vocal Line: Lyrical; mixed conjunct-disjunct (begins *so - do'*)

Tonality: C major (a minor) (Begins *so do'*)

Phrase Structure: Alternating 4 and 5-bar phrases

Texture: Unison voices with piano accompaniment.

Vocal Range:

Time

Meter: Triple

Meter Signature: $\frac{3}{4}$

Conduct: In 3

Tempo: Andante (♩ = ca. 72)

Characteristic Rhythm: Varied

Performance Time: ca. 2′

Text

Source: From the Notebooks for singer Anna Magdalena, Bach's second wife.

Theme: The contentment, joy, and peacefulness of resting ("Ruh").

Pronunciation:

German Word	IPA Symbol *
Bist du bei mir	[bɪs du bɑi mɪə]
geh ich	[ge ɪhch]
mit freunden	[mɪt frɔɪdən]
zum Sterben	[tsʊm shtɛr-bən]
und zu meiner Ruh.	[ʊnht tzu mɑi-nər] [ru]
ach wie	[ahch vi]
vergnügt *	[fər-knykt]
wär so mein	[vɛr zo mɑin]
Ende	[ɛn-də]
es drückten	[ɛs dryk-tən]
deine schönen	[dɑi-nə shø-nən]
Hände	[hɛn-də]
mir die getreunen	[mɪr di gə-troy-ən]
augen zu.	[au-gən tsu]

* [sing (ee) with rounded lips forming (oo)]

- See *Practice Project Four* for English word equivalents.

Form

Ternary AABA; [A (4+5) :‖ B (4+5), (4+5) da capo A (4+5)]

Style

In Baroque style, the eighth note figures [♪♫] and the dotted figures [♪♫ ♪♫] should have a lyrical, but slightly detached articulation.

Social - Historical

Some scholars suggest that Bach wrote this beautiful and famous song for his second wife, Anna Magdalena to sing in 1725. Although the text is associated with endings, its uplifting and lyrical beauty suggests a joyous contentment and happiness. This song is often performed by solo voice and organ. It is heard regularly in times of celebration and passage.

BIST DU BEI MIR

JOHANN SEBASTIAN BACH
Edited & Translated by
Doreen Rao

Rehearsal Guide

Bist du bei mir

> Your ability to perform *Bist du bei mir* requires musicianship. In rehearsal, you will have the opportunity to *produce* the song, *practice* the musicianship necessary to meet the musical challenges, and *perform* with skill and understanding.

The musical challenges of performing this song include your ability to:

- **perform** the lyrical, Baroque style melody with legato yet detached articulations in the eighth-note patterns;

- **prepare** the range demands requiring breath support and open vowel sounds on the highest pitches;

- **sing** both German and English texts (refer to the German pronunciation in the Orientation);

- **convey** the expressive, spiritual quality of the poetry.

Producing

1. **Listen** to the Glen Ellyn Children's Chorus recorded performance of Bach's *Bist du bei mir* (*We Will Sing!* cassette, side 2). **Follow** the score and determine where the singers took a breath to support the long phrases.

2. **Describe** the vocal tone quality of the recorded performance of this song. **Q:** In which language did the Choir perform?

Practicing

1. On a subdivided beat (♩ = ♫), **sing** the first nine bars of the melody using the metric counting system suggested here: (some classes might wish to use the rhythm syllable system instead. **Review** using rhythm syllables in Practice Project Six.)

2. **Sing** the same section once more. This time, "stress" only the first beat of each bar. The other pulses should remain supported, but "unstressed". This contrast in articulation creates a dance-like quality that will help you perform in *Baroque style*.

3. Sing mm. 10-18 using the same metric counting system. (For a review of the metric counting system, refer to Practice Project Six.) Remember to sing the repeated eighth-note patterns with heavy-light (stressed (–), unstressed (˘)) articulations to assure a light, dance-like *Baroque style*.

4. Follow the same procedure in mm. 19-36.

5. If you are performing in English, **sing** the entire [A] section with repeats. If you are preparing to sing in German, **listen** to the Glen Ellyn Children's Chorus recording again (*We Will Sing!* cassette, side 2) and follow the German text in the written score. **Review** the German Pronunciation in the Orientation then **sing** mm. 1-18 in German.

6. When you feel secure with this material and your teacher thinks you are ready to go on, continue from the beginning of the song. Work to improve the tone quality and the rhythmic articulations to match the *Baroque style* of singing. To meet this challenge, prepare each phrase with a full breath, keep the upper body poised to support the tone, and

articulate the consonants in each phrase. (For a review of consonants, see Practice Project Four.)

7. **Listen** to another recorded performance of Bach's famous song, *Bist du bei mir* (see the Selected Recordings list at the end of this Rehearsal Guide.) **Discuss** the qualities of this interpretation.

8. Continue to rehearse *Bist du bei mir* with your class. Since this work can be performed either as a *solo* piece or as an ensemble piece, you may consider practicing it as a soloist or performing it in a small ensemble.

9. You may decide to perform this work in English, German or in both languages.

Performing

1. **Sing** the whole song from beginning to end. Follow your conductor and remember to:

   • **feel** the constant inner pulse as it propels the melodic line forward;

   • **sustain** the lyrical melodic line without singing heavily or flat;

   • **sing** the eighth-note patterns with heavy-light (stressed-unstressed) articulations to assure a light *Baroque style;*

   • **prepare** the high notes in the phrases with full preparatory breaths keeping a high upper body position;

   • **tune** the *accidentals* (altered pitches) to assure good intonation throughout the song. (For a review of accidentals refer to Practice Project Seven.)

Reflecting - Evaluating

You have been learning how to use your singing voice, you have been developing your music reading and counting skills, and you have been studying J.S. Bach's *Bist du bei mir*. In rehearsal, you *produced* the song with your singing voice, you *practiced* the musicianship required to meet the musical challenges, and you *performed* in class or concert. As you review your performance, complete the following reflections for your journal.

1. **Describe** how you used your voice to perform this song.

2. **Describe** your ability to meet the musical challenges in performing artistically.

3. **Describe** how you could improve your performance.

   • As an assessment alternative, you may complete the Self-Evaluation or Concert Critique form to include in your *We Will Sing!* Performance Portfolio.

To improve your musicianship and to perform artistically, you may return to any of the problem-solving exercises as often as you like. It is also recommended that you review the related activities in Practice Project Six, p. 50, p. 52, p. 59 and Practice Project Seven, p. 79-80.

Selected Recordings

We Will Sing! cassette, side 2. Glen Ellyn Children's Chorus. (Recorded in the key of D♭.)

For a solo voice recording of *Bist du bei mir,* listen to Kiri Te Kanawa, on the recording:

Ave Maria. Kiri Te Kanawa, Philips 412 629-2 (also 629-4; LD 629-1).

MY PERFORMANCE PORTFOLIO

Bist du bei Mir

Name:_____ Date:_____

Self - Evaluation

1. **Describe** your performance of *Bist du bei mir.*

   a. Did you sing in *Baroque style?*

2. **Describe** what you did to achieve a *Baroque style* performance.

3. In what language did you perform?

4. **Compare** and **contrast** the quality of your diction with the Glen Ellyn Children's Chorus recording?

5. **Explain** how you produced an expressive performance.

6. **Describe** the quality of your intonation. How could you improve it for future performances?

7. **Explain** what you enjoyed most in the rehearsal and performance of this song.

8. **Review** your performance of *Bist du bei mir* on audio or video cassette. Decide what you like most about your performance and what you would like to improve.

Orientation

Ching-a-ring Chaw
Minstrel Song
arr. Aaron Copland (1900 - 1990)

Pitch

Vocal Line: Mainly chordal melody outlining basic harmonic progression I, IV, V, I.

Tonality: D major (Begins on *so*)

Phrase Structure: 4-bar phrases

Texture: Unison voices and piano accompaniment

Vocal Range:

Time

Meter: Duple

Meter Signature: $\frac{2}{4}$

Conduct: In 2

Tempo: Lively ♩ = ca.120

Characteristic Rhythm:

Performance Time: 2′ 30″

Text

Source: Harris Collection of American poetry and plays

Theme: Strumming and preaching 'bout the promised land

Form

Rondo or expanded ternary form: AB AB A. The "Ching-a-ring" Rondo theme repeats with variations between each episode. The final "Ching-a-ring" Rondo theme takes the form of an extended coda lasting ten bars. [Intro (4), Rondo theme (8), episode (8+8+8), Rondo theme (8), episode (8+8), interlude (8), episode (8), Rondo theme, coda (10)]

Style

Contemporary; popular style and rhythmic

Social - Historical

Aaron Copland is recognized as a leading voice in contemporary American music. He was a mentor and friend to the late American conductor Leonard Bernstein. In his arrangement of the Minstrel song, *Ching-a-ring Chaw*, Copland makes use of the popular style and rhythmic pattern-making that grows naturally from the sights and sounds of rural America. In this appealing song, the short rhythms suggest speech patterns and the instrumental plucking sounds of banjo playing, characteristics of the minstrel style.

CHING-A-RING CHAW

Minstrel Song

Arranged by
AARON COPLAND

The words for this song have been adapted from the original, in the Harris Collection of American Poetry and Plays in Brown University.

Rehearsal Guide

Ching-a-ring Chaw

Your ability to perform *Ching-a-ring Chaw* requires musicianship. In rehearsal, you will have the opportunity to *produce* the song, *practice* the musicianship necessary to meet the musical challenges, and *perform* with skill and understanding.

The musical challenges of performing this song include your ability to:

- **perform** with an understanding of Rondo form as it organizes the minstrel strumming themes and story episodes of this old American song;

- **feel** the natural rhythm of the "ching-a-ring" theme in a characteristically country style and at the varying dynamic levels indicated in the score;

- **remember** the text sequence of the three episode sections;

- **tune** the D major chordal melodies, paying close attention to pitch at *mi* (F♯) and *do* (D);

- **support** the rhythmically augmented cadences on *do* (D) which vary slightly at the end of each section.

Producing

1. Call out the natural spoken rhythm of these words at the varying dynamic levels indicated. Speak in a rhythmic style:

   mf
   Ching-a-ring-a ring ching ching
   Ho-a ding-a ding kum larkee
   (mm. 5-14)

   mp
   Ching-a-ring-a ring ching
   ching-a ring ching, Ho-a ding-a ding kum larkee
   (mm. 48-56)

   p
   Ching-a-ring ching ching,
   ching-a-ring-a, ching-a-ring-a
   f ═══════════════ *ff*
   Ring ching ching ching Chaw!
   (mm. 97-106)

2. **Listen** to the Glen Ellyn Children's Chorus recorded performance of *Ching-a-ring Chaw* on the *We Will Sing!* cassette, side 2. **Listen** for the repeated "ching-a-ring" Rondo theme, and **identify** how many times this theme is heard in Copland's arrangement.

Practicing

1. **Solfege** the pitch pattern:

   s   m   d   s

2. **Solfege** the next pitch pattern:

   l   f   l   d'

3. **Sing** the first rondo theme with text (mm. 5-13).

4. **Sing** the next rondo theme with text (mm. 48-56).

5. **Compare** and **contrast** these two rondo themes.

6. **Sing** the final rondo themes at mm. 97-106. **Compare** and **contrast** this section with the first two rondo themes.

7. **Chant** the natural rhythm of the text in the last four bars (mm. 103-106). **Identify** the distinguishing rhythmic feature at m. 103. **Q:** How long is the rest value in m. 103?

8. Find mm. 103 and 104. **Q:** How many times do you sing the text: "ching-a-ring-a"?

9. **Chant** the text of the last two bars (mm. 105-106). **Observe** the accent over the first beat of each measure.

10. **Sing** the final rondo theme from mm. 97-106. Raise your hand at the quarter-note rest (⁊) in m. 103.

11. Find the first episode at m. 16. Using the Curwen-Kodály handsigns, slowly **solfege** the melody from m. 16 through m. 47. (For a review of the handsigns refer to Practice Project Seven).

12. **Q:** How many different times does the episode material occur in this section of the arrangement? **Q:** What is different? What is the same?

13. Find the last episode in the arrangement. Slowly **solfege** the melody form m. 58 through m. 95.

14. **Q:** What musical elements change in these statements of the final episode?

15. Return to the first episode beginning at m. 16 and **sing** the entire section with text. Continue with the second episode beginning at m. 58 and **sing** with text.

Performing

1. **Sing** the entire song with text throughout. Follow your conductor and remember to:

   • **prepare** each new section with a full preparatory breath;

   • **interpret** the old American Minstrel song using clear diction and rhythmic singing;

   • **contrast** the rondo theme sections with the story telling episodes;

   • **memorize** the text of the entire song so you can perform with confidence and style.

Reflecting - Evaluating

You have been learning how to use your singing voice, you have been developing your music reading and counting skills, and you have been studying Aaron Copland's arrangement of the minstrel song *Ching-a-ring Chaw*. In rehearsal, you *produced* the song with your singing voice, you *practiced* the musicianship required to meet the musical challenges, and you *performed* in class or concert. As you review your performance, complete the following reflections for your journal.

1. **Describe** how you used your voice to perform this song.

2. **Describe** your ability to meet the musical challenges in performing artistically.

3. **Describe** how you could improve your performance.

   • As an assessment alternative, you may complete the Self-Evaluation or Concert Critique form to include in your *We Will Sing!* Performance Portfolio.

To improve your musicianship and to perform artistically, you may return to any of the problem-solving exercises as often as you like. It is also recommended that you review the related activities in Practice Project Six, p. 149.

Selected Recordings

We Will Sing! cassette, side 2. Glen Ellyn Children's Chorus.

A solo voice performance of *Ching-a-Ring Chaw*, accompanied by piano may be heard on:

Old American Songs I and II. Roberta Alexander, soprano; Roger Vignoles, piano. Etcetera KTC 1100.

A solo voice performance, accompanied by orchestra, may be heard on:

Tribute to Aaron Copland. Bruce Hubbard, baritone; The Orchestra of Saint Luke's, Dennis Russell Davies, conductor. EMI CDC 54282.

MY PERFORMANCE PORTFOLIO
Ching-a-Ring Chaw

Name:_____ Date:_____

Self - Evaluation

1. **Describe** your performance of *Ching-a-Ring Chaw.*

    1a. Did you sing with rhythmic definition and pitch accuracy?

2. **Describe** the Rondo form in the Minstrel song, *Ching-a-ring Chaw.*

3. **Explain** what you enjoyed most in the rehearsal and performance of this song.

4. **Review** your performances o *Ching-a-ring Chaw* on audio or video cassette. **Decide** what you like about your performance and what you would like to improve.

PERFORMANCE PROJECTS

Program Three

Orientation

"Hodie" from A Ceremony of Carols, Opus 28
Benjamin Britten (1913 – 1976)

Pitch

Vocal Line: Plainsong melody; unmeasured; stepwise motion

Tonality: A major (Begins on *do*)

Phrase Structure: Irregular

Texture: Unison voices, (harp or piano when processional is not possible)

Vocal Range:

Time

Meter: Unmetered

Meter Signature: *Senza misura*

Conduct: Mixed patterns or freely

Tempo: (♩ = 138)

Characteristic Rhythm: Natural rhythm of text

Performance Time: Ad lib. if processing (45″ if performed straight)

Text

Source: Latin; traditional Medieval text; liturgical; common text used in many Renaissance motets.

Theme: A joyous celebration;

> *...on this day, the angels sing, rejoice.*
> *gloria in excelsis Deo. Alleluia,*

Pronunciation:

Latin Text	IPA Symbols
Hodie,	[ˈhodie]
Christus	[kristus]
natus est	[natus ɛst]
Hodie Salvator	[ˈhodie, saLvatɔɣ]
apparuit.	[apparuit]
Hodie in terra	[ˈhodie, in tɛrra]
canunt, angeli	[kanʊnt, andʒLi]
Laetantur, archangeli	[LetantUr, arkandʒLi]
Hodie, exsultant	[ˈhodie, ɛxuLtant]
justi dicentes	[justi, ditʃɛntɛs]
gloria in excelsis,	[gLɔria in ɛxtʃɛLsɪs]
Deo, Alleluia.	[deo, aLLeLuia]

Form

Phrasing follows text. *A Ceremony of Carols* is a cycle of nine separate Medieval carols framed by the Processional "Hodie", brought back as a Recessional; free-style plainchant used to process and recess in concert.

Style

Although Britten's writing is contemporary, this plainsong melody recreates a sense of the early Medieval chant associated with early musics. "Hodie" can be performed as a concert processional, an opening on stage, or as both processional and recessional.

Social - Historical

Composed in 1942 during World War II as Benjamin Britten returned to England from the United States. *A Ceremony of Carols* is considered to be one of the composer's most popular works. The work was first performed by Fleet Street Choir under the direction of T.B. Lawrence. Since that time, it is performed regularly by boychoirs, children's choirs, and school choirs. The Medieval carols combine with the contemporary harmonies to create a mystical and appealing experience.

For Ursula Nettleship

HODIE

from A CEREMONY OF CAROLS

BENJAMIN BRITTEN
Op. 28

Accompaniment to be played only when an actual procession is impossible.

* The last two bars to be repeated when the duration of procession necessitates.

Rehearsal Guide

"Hodie" from A Ceremony of Carols

Your ability to perform *"Hodie" from A Ceremony of Carols* requires musicianship. In rehearsal, you will have the opportunity to *produce* the song, *practice* the musicianship necessary to meet the musical challenges, and *perform* with skill and understanding.

The musical challenges of performing this song include your ability to:

• **tune** the ascending melody *do - re - mi* ;

• **sing** in a legato, free rhythmic style suggested naturally by the text setting;

• **sustain** pure vowel sounds over two or more notes in the melody;

• **convey** the joyful character of the text.

Producing

1. **Listen** to the Glen Ellyn Children's Chorus sing " Hodie" (*We Will Sing!* cassette, side 2). As you listen, follow the contour of the melody line with your finger. Did you notice the smooth, legato quality of the plainsong melody?

Practicing

1. **Chant** the Latin text in free rhythm noting which syllables receive stress. (You can review the Latin pronunciation in the " Hodie" Orientation.)

Hodie Christus natus est:
hodie Salvator apparuit:
hodie in terra canunt angeli:
letantur archangeli:

hodie exsultant justi dicentes:
gloria in excelsis Deo.
Alleluia!

2. Make sure that you are keeping the vowels pure as you **chant** the text. For a review of vocal phonetics, refer to Practice Project Four.

3. As your teacher guides you, **sing** the first five measures of "Hodie." Each "Hodie" statement in this section is based on the first four notes of the A major scale.

d   r   m   f

Identify where the melody moves to a new position. **Sing** this section beginning at m. 6. **Identify** where the melody moves back to its initial postion. **Sing** the last two lines, beginning at m. 7.

4. **Q:** How many times does the word "hodie" appear in the text? **Sing** each phrase beginning with "hodie" and **compare** pitch relationships between sections.

5. Refer to Practice Project Seven for a review of tonic solfa. **Q:** Which pitch is *do?* **Q:** Which pitch is repeated most?

6. **Sing** the fourth phrase beginning with "hodie" using tonic solfa. (The first pitch is *mi.*) Are you making sure that the *fi* (D♯) is sung higher than *fa* (D♮)? Practice singing these two patterns with handsigns:

7. **Sing** the last two "alleluias." **Q:** Are you capturing the rejoicing spirit of the text? What is the dynamic level for these last two phrases? What is the difference in the way these two "alleluias" are set to music?

8. "Hodie" should be sung freely, not in a strict meter. **Q:** How do you think this piece should be conducted? **Experiment** with different patterns and conducting gestures to illustrate the rhythm of the text and character of the music.

9. **Sing** "Hodie" from the beginning, carefully observing the dynamic markings, especially the crescendo-decrescendo within phrases.

10. "Hodie" was written as a processional. **Sing** while walking slowly single file or in pairs. Remember to maintain a good singing posture as you walk.

11. **Listen** to "This Little Babe," another carol from Britten's *A Ceremony of Carols*, sung by the Glen Ellyn Children's Chorus (*We Will Sing!* cassette, side 2). As you listen, consider the following questions:

    (a) What is the rhythmic character of "This Little Babe?"

    (b) This piece is four verses long. The first three verses are a canon. The first verse is sung in unison, the second verse in two-part canon and the third verse in three-part canon. **Q:** How is the fourth verse different?

    (c) What language is the text?

12. **Compare** and **contrast** the rhythmic and melodic qualities of "This Little Babe" with "Hodie."

Performing

1. **Sing** the whole carol. Follow the conductor and remember to:

- **support** and **sustain** the legato plainsong melody;

- **begin** each phrase with a preparatory breath and **sing** the intervals in tune;

- **shape** the vowels throughout the vocal line;

- **perform** joyfully!

Reflecting - Evaluating

You have been learning how to use your singing voice, you have been developing your music reading and counting skills, and you have been studying Benjamin Britten's "Hodie" from *A Ceremony of Carols*. In rehearsal, you *produced* the song with your singing voice, you *practiced* the musicianship required to meet the musical challenges, and you *performed* in class or concert. As you review your performance, complete the following reflections for your journal.

1. **Describe** how you used your voice to perform this song.

2. **Describe** your ability to meet the musical challenges in performing artistically.

3. **Describe** how you could improve your performance.

    - As an assessment alternative, you may complete the Self-Evaluation or Concert Critique form to include in your *We Will Sing!* Performance Portfolio.

To improve your musicianship and to perform artistically, you may return to any of the problem-solving exercises as often as you like. It is also recommended that you review the related activities in Practice Project Six, p. 57.

Selected Recordings

Excerpts from *A Ceremony of Carols:* "Hodie" and "This Little Babe" are performed by the Glen Ellyn Children's Chorus on the *We Will Sing!* cassette, side 2.

You may enjoy listening to the King's College Choir sing the entire *A Ceremony of Carols* on:

A Ceremony of Carols. Choir of King's College, Cambridge, David Willcocks, conductor. Angel CDC-47709; Seraphim S-60217.

For another recording of Britten's well-known work *A Ceremony of Carols,* you may enjoy listening to a performance recorded by the Texas Boys' Choir.

A Ceremony of Carols. The Gregg Smith Singers and The Texas Boys' Choir, Gregg Smith, conductor. Vox Prima MWCD-1704.

M Y   P E R F O R M A N C E   P O R T F O L I O

"Hodie" from A Ceremony of Carols

Name:_____ Date:_____

Self - Evaluation

1. **Describe** your performance of the "Hodie" from *A Ceremony of Carols*.

   a.Did you sing expressively and in tune?

2. **Review** the challenges listed in the orientation section of the rehearsal guide for "Hodie." Explain how you met each of the challenges as you rehearsed and performed "Hodie".

3. **Compare** and **contrast** your performance of "Hodie" with the Glen Ellyn Children's Chorus recorded version.

4. **Explain** what you enjoyed most in the rehearsal and performance of this plainsong-like melody.

5. **Review** your performance on audio or video cassette. **Decide** what you like about your performance and what you would like to improve.

Orientation

A Child is Born
Anonymous

Pitch

Vocal Line: Chordal melody outlining I-V-I

Tonality: E major (Begins on *do*)

Phrase Structure: Four bars plus six bars

Texture: Unison voices in two, three, four, or five-part canon, unaccompanied

Vocal Range:

Time

Meter: Triple

Meter Signature: ¾

Conduct: In 1 or 3

Tempo: (♩ = ca. 112)

Characteristic Rhythm:

$$\frac{3}{4} \, \downarrow \quad | \quad \downarrow$$

Performance Time: = ad lib.

Text

Source: Unknown

Theme: A carol; song of rejoicing

Form

Organized in two short phrases (A B); in strict canon at the bar.

Style

Contemporary; with bright tone and exact rhythms.

Social - Historical

Since the source is anonymous, its history can begin with your experience.

A CHILD IS BORN

Anon.
arranged by
Doreen Rao

Rehearsal Guide
A Child is Born

> Your ability to perform *A Child is Born* requires musicianship. In rehearsal, you will have the opportunity to *produce* the song, *practice* the musicianship necessary to meet the musical challenges, and *perform* with skill and understanding.

The musical challenges of performing this song include your ability to:

- **support** the octave leap from *do* to *do'* (E - E') accurately;

- **tune** the descending E major scale;

- **convey** the joyful character of the text as expressed in the word "nowell";

- **perform** in two, three, four, or five-part canon.

Producing

1. As your teacher guides you, **sing** the unison canon with text. Remember to maintain good singing posture and begin singing with a preparatory breath.

Practicing

1. **Vocalize** the octave leap *do - do'* in a number of keys beginning on E♭ and moving up by semi-tone to F.

2. **Sing** the E octave interval to the text "nowell." Modify the final [ɛ] vowel of now<u>e</u>ll toward the brighter [e] vowel (Jaw should be dropped, tongue position forward). This vowel modification will ensure good intonation.

3. Referring to Practice Project Seven for review of tonic solfa, **identify** where *do* is written in *A Child is Born*.

4. Beginning on *do'* (E), **sing** a descending major scale using tonic solfa. **Listen** carefully to each pitch and sing lightly as you descend to ensure good intonation.

5. **Q:** What are the tonic solfa syllables for the last two statements of "nowell"? **Sing** this interval using tonic solfa.

6. **Sing** the entire unison carol again. Observe the breath marks (') indicated.

7. **Identify** the meter signature for this canon. **Q:** Should this canon be conducted in three or in one? Why?

8. When you feel ready, and your conductor agrees that your unison singing is secure, you may begin rehearsing *A Child is Born* in canon. Singing in canon creates a texture that is called *polyphony*.

9. **Sing** *A Child is Born* in two, three, four, and five-part canon. Remember to breathe at the beginning of each new phrase.

Performing

1. **Sing** the whole song. Follow your conductor and remember to:

- **keep** a good singing posture;

- **prepare** each phrase with a preparatory breath;

- **listen** carefully for accurate intonation, especially on the octave leap and the descending major scale;

- **perform** expressively and let your "no-well's ring out joyfully.

Reflecting - Evaluating

You have been learning how to use your singing voice, you have been developing your music reading and counting skills, and you have been studying *A Child is Born*. In rehearsal, you *produced* the song with your singing voice, you *practiced* the musicianship required to meet the musical challenges, and you *performed* in class or concert. As you review your performance, complete the following reflections for your journal.

1. **Describe** how you used your voice to perform this song.

2. **Describe** your ability to meet the musical challenges in performing artistically.

3. **Describe** how you could improve your performance.

   - As an assessment alternative, you may complete the Self-Evaluation or Concert Critique form to include in your *We Will Sing!* Performance Portfolio.

To improve your musicianship and to perform artistically, you may return to any of the problem-solving exercises as often as you like. It is also recommended that you review the related activities in Practice Projects One through Seven.

M Y   P E R F O R M A N C E   P O R T F O L I O

A Child is Born

Name:_____ Date:_____

Self - Evaluation

1. **Describe** your performance of *A Child is Born*.

      a. Did you sing this song with a joyful sound?

      b. Did you sing the octave intervals in tune?

      c. Did the tempo remain steady?

      d. Did you sing securely in unison and in canon?

2. **Explain** what you enjoyed most in your rehearsal and performance of this song.

3. **Review** your performance of *A Child is Born* on audio or video cassette. **Decide** what you like about your performance and what you would like to improve.

Orientation

Poor Little Children
Negro Spiritual

Pitch

Vocal Line: Follows contour of G minor chord

Tonality: G dorian (Begins *re - fa - la*)

Phrase Structure: Mostly 4-bar phrases

Texture: Unison voices, unaccompanied

Vocal Range:

Time

Meter: Duple

Meter Signature: ¢ (cut time)

Conduct: In 2

Tempo: ($\downarrow$ = ca. 72)

Characteristic Rhythm:

Performance Time: ca. 1′ 30″

Text

Source: Unknown

Theme: A spiritual lament.

Form

Strophic; five phrases, separated by a short refrain "Yes, Yes"

Style

Expressive; sung freely, not in strict time

Social - Historical

Poor Little Children is an example of an African-American Negro Spiritual. Spirituals developed out of the slavery of pre-Civil War America. Men, women and children were kidnapped from their African homelands and carried across the ocean on overcrowded ships. Once in America, Africans were sold as possessions, made to work long hours, and forced to live in appalling conditions.

Slaves had few personal possessions and were oppressed and often abused. Singing spirituals developed as a way of expressing feelings and offering hope for a better world. Opportunities for social gatherings were limited. Many songs were "coded" and contained messages and meanings known only among the slaves. Since the church was one of the few places that slaves could meet and sing together, many spirituals have religious texts.

Poor Little Children is one of the few spirituals dealing with the subject of the nativity. The text of *Poor Little Children* expresses pity and shame that the children should be born into slavery. The second verse, written especially for young choirs, mourns the fact that many children are still being born into hunger and poverty.

POOR LITTLE CHILDREN

Negro Spiritual
arranged by
Doreen Rao

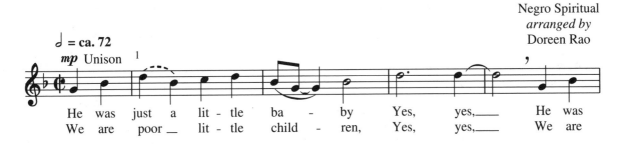

Rehearsal Guide
Poor Little Children

> Your ability to perform *Poor Little Children* requires musicianship. In rehearsal, you will have the opportunity to *produce* the song, *practice* the musicianship necessary to meet the musical challenges, and *perform* with skill and understanding.

The musical challenges of performing this song include your ability to:

- **sing** the ascending and descending dorian melody in tune;

- **feel** the syncopated rhythm of the repeated refrain on the text "Yes, Yes";

- **interpret** the expressive, lamenting character of this spiritual.

Producing

1. Remembering to use your best posture, follow your conductor, and **sing** the first verse of *Poor Little Children.*

Practicing

1. Using the vowel combination (oo)-(ah) **vocalize** the following pattern of the g minor chord.

(oo) _____ (ah) _____

Remember to drop your jaw when you sing the (ah) vowel. Place your index finger on your chin to help you to shape the vowel. (Refer to Practice Project Four for a review of vocal diction.)

2. **Sing** the first verse with text. Remember to prepare the open (ah) vowel for the text "wasn't that" at m. 13.

3. Referring to Practice Project Seven for a review, use the *key signature* to help you find *do.* **Sing** the last two phrases with solfa syllables beginning at m. 13. **Q:** How can you prepare the beginning of each phrase so that *re* (G) is sung in tune?

4. The meter signature of *Poor Little Children* is ¢ or ²₂. **Q:** How many beats will you feel in each measure? Keeping the beat, sing the first twelve measures. **Q:** Can you find an example of *syncopation?* (Refer to Practice Project Six for a review of syncopation.)

5. **Sing** from m. 13 to the end. **Chant** the text and **clap** the rhythm of any syncopated rhythms that you find in the last two phrases of the song.

6. Following your conductor, **sing** the second verse of *Poor Little Children.* Remember to use your best posture and to sing the words expressively. **Q:** How is the second verse similar to the first verse? How is it different?

7. **Sing** verse two of *Poor Little Children,* keeping a strict, steady beat. (You may enjoy playing a tambourine to keep the steady beat.) **Q:** What suggestions can you make for a more expressive performance?

8. **Sing** both verses following your conductor in a relaxed rhythmic style.

9. Quite often, spirituals are sung in a *call and response* form, with a soloist or small group singing a phrase, answered by the whole group. **Experiment** with performing *Poor Little Children* in call and response form. Choose one person or a small group to sing the first phrase: "He was just a little baby." The rest of the choir sings the syncopated refrain: "Yes, yes." Continue in this manner for the next two phrases. Everyone sings "Wasn't it a pity and a shame" (tutti).

10. Using the form of *Poor Little Children* to guide you, **write** your own third verse for this spiritual. **Write** about something that you feel is a "pity and a shame." **Perform** your own verse for the rest of the choir. Record your performance for your Performance Portfolio.

Performing

1. Following the conductor, **sing** the whole spiritual. Remember to:

   • **begin** each phrase with a preparatory breath;

   • **observe** the dynamics indicated in the written score;

   • **sing** with a relaxed, rhythmic style;

   • **feel** the syncopated rhythms on the texts "Yes, yes" and "pity and a shame."

Reflecting - Evaluating

You have been learning how to use your singing voice, you have been developing your music reading and counting skills, and you have been studying the Negro Spiritual *Poor Little Children*. In rehearsal, you *produced* the song with your singing voice, you *practiced* the musicianship required to meet the musical challenges, and you *performed* in class or concert. As you review your performance, complete the following reflections for your journal.

1. **Describe** how you used your voice to perform this song.

2. **Describe** your ability to meet the musical challenges in performing artistically.

3. **Describe** how you could improve your performance.

   • As an assessment alternative, you may complete the Self-Evaluation or Concert Critique form to include in your *We Will Sing!* Performance Portfolio.

To improve your musicianship and to perform artistically, you may return to any of the problem-solving exercises as often as you like. It is also recommended that you review the related activities in Practice Projects One through Seven.

Selected Recordings

Other examples of spirituals sung by world famous solo artists Kathleen Battle, Jessye Norman, and Leontyne Price may be found on *Spirituals in Concert* and *Swing Low, Sweet Chariot*.

Spirituals in Concert. Kathleen Battle and Jessye Norman, James Levine, conductor. Deutsche Grammophon DG 429 790-2.

Swing Low, Sweet Chariot. Leontyne Price, soprano. RCA LSC-2600.

Choral arrangements of spirituals are performed by the Tuskagee Institute Choir and the Robert Shaw Chorale.

Spirituals. Tuskagee Institute Choir, William L. Dawson, director. Westminster WST 14989.

I'm Goin' to Sing. The Robert Shaw Chorale, Robert Shaw, conductor. LSC 2580.

M Y   P E R F O R M A N C E   P O R T F O L I O

Poor Little Children

Name:_____ Date:_____

Self - Evaluation

1. **Describe** your performance of *Poor Little Children*.

    a. Did you sing expressively and in tune?

    b. Were you able to express the meaning of the text?

    c. Did you articulate the syncopated rhythms?

    d. Did you sing in a relaxed, rhythmic style?

2. **Review** your performance of *Poor Little Children* on audio or video cassette. **Decide** what you like about your performance and what you would like to improve.

Orientation

"How Beautiful are the Feet of Them" from Messiah
George Frederick Handel
(1685 – 1759)

Pitch

Vocal Line: Conjunct, mostly stepwise movement; each phrase begins with a leap

Tonality: G minor (Begins *mi - do*)

Phrase Structure: Mostly 2-bar phrases

Texture: Unison voices, keyboard accompaniment

Vocal Range:

Time

Meter: Compound duple

Meter Signature: $\frac{12}{8}$

Conduct: In 4

Tempo: Larghetto (♩ = ca. 132)

Characteristic Rhythm:

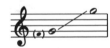

Performance Time: 2′ 40″

Text

Source: The Old Testament; Romans 10:15

Theme: Joy in hearing of peace

Form

Binary; two asymmetrical sections with keyboard introduction, interlude, and coda.

Style

In Baroque style; the dotted figures should have a lyrical but slightly detached articulation.

Social - Historical

"How Beautiful are the Feet of Them" is from Part Three of Handel's Oratorio, *Messiah*. Handel wrote the entire oratorio in just twenty-four days. The first performance was a charity concert in Dublin, Ireland, on April 13, 1742. *Messiah* is the most frequently performed oratorio in the world. An *oratorio* is a dramatic work which employs arias, recitatives, ensembles, choruses, and instrumental music. Unlike opera, oratorio is not intended to be staged.

There are many well-known arias and choruses from *Messiah*. The best known is probably the "Hallelujah Chorus." You may enjoy listening to the "Hallelujah Chorus" on one of the popular recordings listed at the end of this Rehearsal Guide. " How Beautiful are the Feet of Them" was written as an aria for soprano, violins, and continuo.

George Frederick Handel was born in Germany in 1685. After studying and composing in Germany and Italy, he settled in London, England, in 1712. He wrote numerous operas and oratorios as well as vocal and instrumental chamber music and works for orchestra.

HOW BEAUTIFUL ARE THE FEET OF THEM

from MESSIAH

for Unison Treble Voices & Piano

Romans 10:15

GEORGE FREDERICK HANDEL

Edited by Doreen Rao

* optional ending

Rehearsal Guide

"How Beautiful are the Feet of Them" from Messiah

Your ability to perform "How Beautiful are the Feet of Them" requires musicianship. In rehearsal, you will have the opportunity to *produce* the song, *practice* the musicianship necessary to meet the musical challenges, and *perform* with skill and understanding.

The musical challenges of performing this song include your ability to:

- **support** the sustained, legato line with the breath; **shape** the pure vowel sounds;

- **tune** the descending melody in g minor; intervals of a minor seventh and octave leaps at the beginning of phrases; **sustain** the lilt of ⅞ (compound duple time);

- **interpret** the lyrical Baroque-style melody with legato, yet detached articulations in the dotted rhythm figures;

- **negate** the "r" in the word "are"; roll the "r" in the word "bring";

- **perform** the poetic text with good vocal diction.

Producing

1. Following the score, **listen** to the Glen Ellyn Children's Chorus recording of "How Beautiful are the Feet of Them" on the *We Will Sing!* cassette, side 2.

Practicing

1. **Chant** the text:

    "How beautiful are the feet of them
    that preach the gospel of peace."

Strive to keep the vowels pure, especially the (ah) vowel in the diphthong of the word "how", and the (oo) vowel in the diphthong of the word "beautiful" (this is the same sound as in "m<u>u</u>sic"). Refer to *Practice Project Four* for a review of vocal phonetics.

2. **Vocalize** the opening pitches of the melody on the neutral syllable "no."

    no - no - no - no - no - no - no

3. **Listen** to the 4-bar piano introduction and **sing** the opening vocal material, mm. 5-9. **Q:** What part of the melody do you hear in the piano introduction? How many times do you sing the text "How Beautiful are the Feet" in mm. 5-9? **Describe** the varying shape of the melodic line each time you sing this text.

4. As your teacher guides you, **prepare** your breath and **sing** the opening phrase once again. Think carefully about where you will breathe. **Q:** How many phrases are there in the material from mm. 5-9? Can you sing the first 2-bar phrase in one breath?

5. **Q:** What vowel do you hear in the word "are"? When you sing this word, sustain the (ah) vowel and leave off the "r."

6. Following your conductor, **listen** to the piano interlude at m. 10. **Sing** from m. 11 to the end. Do not move until the piano has finished playing its closing material (called a *coda*). **Q:** Do you hear any material in the interlude or coda which appears elsewhere in the aria?

7. **Compare** and **contrast** the melody in the opening of the second section at m. 11 with the opening of the first section at m. 5. **Q:** How is it the same? How is it different?

8. **Chant** the text "and bring glad tidings" in the rhythm at m. 13. **Chant** the same text at m. 16. **Identify** the vowel color in the first syllable of the word *tidings*. Be sure that you sing on the (ah) part of the diphthong as you sing this syllable over several notes.

9. The "r" in the word "bring" is different than the "r" at the end of the word "are." Practice rolling your "r," then **chant** the text "and bring glad tidings" with a rolled "r." **Sing** from m. 13 to the end of the aria remembering to sing on the (ah) of the word "tidings" and to roll the "r" of the word "bring."

10. Refer to Practice Project Six for a review of meter signatures. **Identify** the meter of "How Beautiful are the Feet of Them." **Q:** Which conducting pattern could you use to conduct this piece?

11. **Listen** to a recording of the chorus "For Unto us a Child is Born" from Handel's *Messiah*. **Describe** the similarities and differences which you notice between these two pieces from *Messiah*.

Performing

1. **Sing** the whole song with keyboard accompaniment. As you follow your conductor remember to:

   • **begin** each phrase with a preparatory breath:

   • **sing** legato phrases;

   • **sing** on pure vowels; avoid early diphthongs;

   • **negate** the "r" at word endings.

Reflecting — Evaluating

You have been learning how to use your singing voice, you have been developing your music reading and counting skills, and you have been studying George Frederick Handel's "How Beautiful are the Feet of Them" from *Messiah*. In rehearsal, you *produced* the song with your singing voice, you *practiced* the musicianship required to meet the musical challenges, and you *performed* in class or concert. As you review your performance, complete the following reflections for your journal.

1. **Describe** how you used your voice to perform this song.

2. **Describe** your ability to meet the musical challenges in performing artistically.

3. **Describe** how you could improve your performance.

   • As an assessment alternative, you may complete the Self-Evaluation or Concert Critique form to include in your *We Will Sing!* Performance Portfolio.

> To improve your musicianship and to perform artistically, you may return to any of the problem-solving exercises as often as you like. It is also recommended that you review the related activities in Practice Projects One through Seven.

Selected Recordings

"How Beautiful are the Feet of Them" is performed by the Glen Ellyn Children's Chorus on the *We Will Sing!* cassette, side 2.

A solo performance of the aria "How beautiful are the feet" may be heard on many recordings of G.F. Handel's *Messiah*. Here are two popular recordings.

For a performance by an American symphony orchestra and chorus you may listen to:

Messiah. The Chicago Symphony Orchestra and Chorus, Sir Georg Solti, conductor. London 414 396-1 (-2;-4).

A performance on authentic period instruments is conducted by Trevor Pinnock, performed by the English Concert Choir and Orchestra.

Messiah. English Concert Choir, The English Concert, Trevor Pinnock, conductor. Deutsche Grammophon DG 423 630-2.

M Y   P E R F O R M A N C E   P O R T F O L I O

"How Beautiful are the Feet of Them"

Name:_____ Date:_____

Self - Evaluation

1. **Describe** your performance of "How Beautiful are the Feet of Them."

    a. Did you sing expressively and in tune?

    b. Did you sing in Baroque style?

2. **Describe** what you did to achieve a Baroque-style performance.

3. **Explain** what you enjoyed most about your rehearsal and performance of this piece.

4. **Compare** and **contrast** your performance of "How Beautiful are the Feet of Them" to the Glen Ellyn Children's Chorus recorded version.

5. **Review** you performance of "How Beautiful are the Feet of Them" on audio or video cassette. **Decide** what you like about your performance and what you would like to improve.

Orientation

In Dulci Jubilo

arr. J.S. Bach (1685 – 1750)

Pitch

Vocal Line: Mostly conjunct, stepwise movement

d r m f s l

Tonality: F major; built on the *hexachord* (F-D) (Begins on *do*)

Phrase Structure: 4-bar phrases, repeated phrases

Texture: Unison voices, keyboard accompaniment

Vocal Range:

Time

Meter: Triple

Meter Signature: ¾

Conduct: In 1 or 3

Tempo: (♩· = ca. 56)

Characteristic Rhythm:

Performance Time: 2′ 20″

Text

Source: German carol, translated by Roland L. De Pearsall (English madrigal composer)

Theme: A carol; a song of rejoicing; "In Dulci Jubilo" means "in sweet joy."

Pronunciation:

Latin Word	IPA Symbol
In dulci jubilo	[in duLtʃi jubiLo]
In praesepio	[in presepio]
Matris in gremio	[matris in gremio]
alpha es et o	[aLfa ɛs ɛt o]
Ubi sunt gaudia	[ubi sənt gaudia]
Nova cantica	[nova kantiKa]
In Regis curia	[in redʒis Kuria]

Form

Strophic form with three verses.

Style

In Baroque style; lyrical, but light.

Social - Historical

In Dulci Jubilo is a German carol from the fourteenth century. Carols are folk-like melodies of a joyful nature. The word "carol" originally meant "to dance in a ring." Many carols still have this dance-like quality. *In Dulci Jubilo* is an example of a *macaronic* carol. In a macaronic form, lines of text in Latin are interspersed with lines in English. Legend has it that the original text and melody were given by a band of angels to Heinrich Suso, a fourteenth century mystic. Composers throughout the ages have written both choral and instrumental arrangements of the carol *In Dulci Jubilo*. This version is arranged by the renowned composer J.S. Bach. Bach wrote many works for choir, as well as works for organ and solo instruments and ensembles. He was also a celebrated organist and choir director. Bach taught at the Thomas-Schule in Leipzig, Germany for many years.

IN DULCI JUBILO

English Translation by
R. L. DePEARSALL

Harmonized by
JOHANN SEBASTIAN BACH
Arranged and edited by
Doreen Rao

Rehearsal Guide

In Dulci Jubilo

> Your ability to perform *In Dulci Jubilo* requires musicianship. In rehearsal, you will have the opportunity to *produce* the song, *practice* the musicianship necessary to meet the musical challenges, and *perform* with skill and understanding.

The musical challenges of performing this song include your ability to:

- **sing** the dance-like melody built on the first six notes of the major scale (hexachord);

- **sustain** the pure vowel sounds of the Latin and English text;

- **convey** the joyful character of the fourteenth century German carol.

Producing

1. Follow the written score while you **listen** to the Glen Ellyn Children's Chorus sing *In Dulci Jubilo* on the *We Will Sing!* cassette, side 2.

Practicing

1. **Sing** the following melodic pattern on the solfa syllables given in the key of F major. These six notes form the basis for most of the melody of *In Dulci Jubilo*.

d   r   m   f   s   l

2. Referring to Practice Project Seven as a review, use the key signature in the score to find *do*. **Sing** the first two phrases to tonic solfa. **Compare** the melody of the first two phrases.

3. **Chant** the text "In dulci jubilo," stressing beginning consonants and pure vowels. **Sing** the first two phrases with text.

4. **Chant** the Latin text beginning at m. 13, then **sing** the whole first verse.

5. Repeat the last two phrases: "Alpha es et O." **Compare** and **contrast** these melodic ideas.

6. **Sing** the last two phrases once again. If your intonation needs to improve, **solfege** the last six measures.

7. **Sing** the entire melody on the repeated syllable "noo" [u]. Remember to support the tone on the breath and work for a rich, warm vocal color.

8. **Identify** the rhythm that occurs most frequently in this carol. **Clap** the first four measures of the carol. **Clap** musically to direct the light, dance-like movement toward the end of the phrase. **Sing** the opening phrase of the carol on the (oo) vowel [u] while drawing the shape of the phrase in the air. Remember to give your phrase direction and shape.

9. **Chant** the Latin text for verse two in rhythm, concentrating on beginning consonants and pure vowels. **Sing** verse two remembering to use your best singing posture.

10. **Sing** both verses with accompaniment.

11. **Listen** to a recording selected from one of Bach's many arrangements of *In Dulci Jubilo* for organ. **Q: Discuss** how Bach uses the carol melody you have been singing.

Performing

1. **Sing** the whole song with piano or organ accompaniment. As you follow your conductor, remember to:

- **begin** each phrase with a preparatory breath;

- **support** the tone on the breath and work for a rich, warm vocal color;

- **articulate** the light, dance-like rhythms;

- **listen** carefully to the intonation, especially at the cadence points;

- **give** each phrase direction and shape.

Reflecting - Evaluating

You have been learning how to use your singing voice, you have been developing your music reading and counting skills, and you have been studying J.S. Bach's *In Dulci Jubilo*. In rehearsal, you *produced* the song with your singing voice, you *practiced* the musicianship required to meet the musical challenges, and you *performed* in class or concert. As you review your performance, complete the following reflections for your journal.

1. **Describe** how you used your voice to perform this song.

2. **Describe** your ability to meet the musical challenges in performing artistically.

3. **Describe** how you could improve your performance.

   - As an assessment alternative, you may complete the Self-Evaluation or Concert Critique form to include in your *We Will Sing!* Performance Portfolio.

To improve your musicianship and to perform artistically, you may return to any of the problem-solving exercises as often as you like. It is also recommended that you review the related activities in Practice Projects One through Seven.

Selected Recordings

J.S. Bach's arrangement of *In Dulci Jubilo* by the Glen Ellyn Children's Chorus on the *We Will Sing!* cassette, side 2.

An SATB choral arrangement of *In Dulci Jubilo,* arranged by Roland L. De Pearsall may be heard on:

Christmas Carols from King's College, Cambridge. The Choir of King's College, Cambridge, David Willcocks and Philip Ledger, conductors. EMI CDC 747500-2.

Many composers have used the melody of the carol *In Dulci Jubilo* as a theme in instrumental works. Bach's chorale prelude for organ, BWV 608, based on this carol, is performed by Marie Claire Alain on:

Das Orgelbuchlein. Marie Claire Alain, organ. Erato EPR 15501.

M Y P E R F O R M A N C E P O R T F O L I O

In Dulci Jubilo

Name:_____ Date:_____

Self - Evaluation

1. **Describe** your performance of *In Dulci Jubilo*.

    a. Did you sing in a legato and dance-like manner?

    b. Were you able to convey the joyful character of this carol?

2. **Explain** what you enjoyed most about your rehearsal and performance of this piece.

3. **Compare** and **contrast** your performance of *In Dulci Jubilo* to the Glen Ellyn Children's Chorus recorded version.

4. **Review** your performance of *In Dulci Jubilo* on audio or video casette. **Decide** what you like about your performance and what you would like to improve.

Orientation

Jingle Bell Swing
Traditional tune
arr. David J. Elliott

Pitch

Vocal Line: Familiar melody, disjunct, some scat singing

Tonality: B♭ major: vocal line anchors on *do* (B♭) and *so* (F)

Phrase Structure: Traditional 4-bar phrases with several 5-bar "twists" in swing style

Texture: Primarily unison with some two-part *divisi*, piano accompaniment or jazz combo of drum set, keyboard, and bass.

Vocal Range:

Time

Meter: 3 + 2

Meter Signature: $\frac{5}{4}$

Conduct: In 2 or 5

In the two-pattern conductors show a longer beat one (three eighth-note pulses) followed by shorter beat two (two eighth-note pulses). In five, conduct in a "jazz style"; keeping time. Avoid traditional conducting style.

Tempo: (♩ = 144)

Characteristic Rhythm:

Performance Time: 1′ 25″

Text

Source: Secular carol

Theme: Festive holiday

Form

Verse form; irregular phrase structure: [4-bar intro, Verse 1: (4 + 4 + 5 + 5 + 2), Verse 2: (4 + 4 + 5 + 4 + 4), 1-bar tag]

Style

The tune is written in "swing" style where eighth notes are performed as "swing" eighths.

Social - Historical

American jazz is a musical practice characterized by many different styles such as swing, be-bop, fusion, blues, and Dixieland. Jazz music, like classical music, is highly structured. Jazz is an indigenous American musical practice with its own structures, performance practices, and styles. This swing tune is an arrangement of a traditional secular carol. The choice of $\frac{5}{4}$ meter reflects the playfulness of the text.

JINGLE BELL SWING

Jingle Bell Swing is one of several holiday songs that make up *Christmas Lites* (Boosey & Hawkes Octavo 6685), a jazz suite commissioned by the Glen Ellyn Children's Chorus. It was premiered December 9, 1991 at Chicago's Orchestra Hall as part of the GECC's program for the annual Margaret Hillis Fellowship concert with the Chicago Symphony Chorus.

Conducting Suggestions

1. As practiced by jazz musicians, the eighth notes in this piece should be performed as "swing eighths":

2. Conduct in a small, unobtrusive pattern. Aim for a light rhythmic feel. (Large conducting gestures will slow the tempo and cause a sluggish feel.)

3. This piece may be conducted in five, or in two (3 + 2). Use the conducting pattern that achieves the lightest rhythmic feel from the chorus. If a two-beat pattern is selected, help the singers feel the longer first beat (1 - 2 - 3) followed by the shorter second beat (4 - 5).

4. Three additional strategies may help in teaching and learning this piece:
    a. Teach the singers how to conduct the pattern.
    b. Sing the entire piece on scat syllables (do-bee-do) until the feel of the swing eighth notes is established.
    c. Play a recording of "Take Five" by the Dave Brubeck Quartet (*Time Out* Columbia CJ 40585) for comparison with the "5" feel of this piece.

5. The last two bars are in **4/4**. The rhythmic pattern in these two bars is the "signature" that Count Basie often used to end his pieces. You may want to listen to recordings by Basie to hear examples of this pattern and the many variations he made upon it.

6. In general, aim for crisp articulation of the words and scat syllables.

7. Scat syllables: do   long, as in too
                        dit   short, as in sit!
                        dah   short, with a heavy accent, as in dot!

8. Accents: strong accent, full value

                   heavy accent, full value!

                   very short, staccato

For the Glen Ellyn Children's Chorus
Sandra Prodan, Music Director

JINGLE BELL SWING

for Two-Part Treble Voices & Piano

Arranged by
DAVID J. ELLIOTT

Piano

All voices in unison

Dash-ing through the snow in a one horse o – pen sleigh

O'er the fields we go Laugh-ing all the way. Bells on bob tails ring, O__

Rehearsal Guide
Jingle Bell Swing 🔘◦

> Your ability to perform *Jingle Bell Swing* requires musicianship. In rehearsal, you will have the opportunity to *produce* the song, *practice* the musicianship necessary to meet the musical challenges, and *perform* with skill and understanding.

The musical challenges of performing this song include your ability to:

- **perform** the uneven "feel" of the Jingle Bell carol arrangement. Feel a long pulse (three eighth-notes) followed by a shorter pulse (two eighth-notes);

- **perform** the eighth notes in "swing" style (♩♪);

- **tune** the descending stepwise motion of the alto line at the refrain (optional);

- **sing** the added scat syllables in verse two;

- **prepare** the dynamic and melodic change of the extended refrain beginning at m. 42.

Producing

1. **Listen** to the Glen Ellyn Children's Chorus sing Elliott's two-part arrangement of the familiar tune *Jingle Bell Swing* (*We Will Sing!* cassette, side 2). **Listen** for the way the original tune is altered. Pay close attention to the jazzy feel of the arrangement.

Practicing

1. With your teacher guiding you, **sing** the first verse and refrain of *Jingle Bell Swing* through m. 23 in the following manner:

   (a) **Identify** where the first verse ends and the refrain begins;

   (b) **Identify** the number of measures in the piano introduction;

   (c) **Sing** the first verse in unison;

   (d) **Sing** just the melody of the refrain.

2. **Chant** the text of verse one, emphasizing the accents marked in the score.

3. **Identify** the meter signature of the arrangement. Discuss the division of beats into the long-short pattern.

4. **Chant** the text of verse one again. **Clap** on the two main pulses of each measure.

   (1 2 3 **4** 5)

       >   >

5. **Read** the notation of the first word, "dashing." **Q:** What note values are written? In a jazz swing, the musician must understand the musical practice by reading even eighth-notes as uneven. **Chant** the first phrase substituting the uneven swing feel (♩♪) for an even eighth-note rhythm.

6. **Describe** the number of verses and refrains that comprise this piece. **Identify** the number of measures in the interlude between the first refrain and the beginning of verse two.

7. **Examine** the use of scat syllables in verse two. Scat singing is usually a spontaneous improvisation where the "flavor" of the passage is important, but the specific syllables chosen are not. When singing in a chorus, however, agreement on specific syllables becomes necessary. **Chant** verse two, experimenting with these syllables. **Sing** verse two and feel free to **move** your body with the music.

8. **Identify** the lower, or alto, part in the first refrain beginning at m. 16. Using your finger, follow the direction of the line. **Q:** Are the pitches moving up or down? **Sing** the refrain of verse two at m. 33, including the four-bar ending. **Examine** the dynamic marking at m. 42 and make the necessary adjustments to your singing.

9. **Discuss** the style of *Jingle Bell Swing*. **Q:** How is it different from singing Lowell Mason's *O Music, Sweet Music* or Bach's *Bist du bei mir?*

10. **Explore** the effect of diction in this style. **Q:** Should consonants be exaggerated or muted?

11. **Q:** How might one achieve energy and intensity within a controlled piano-forte dynamic?

Performing

1. **Sing** the entire piece. Follow the conductor and remember to:

   • **sing** within the style, lightly and with energy;

   • **swing** the eighth notes, accenting the first eighth note of each pattern as marked;

   • **mute** the consonants for a natural, easy feel;

   • feel comfortable in allowing your body to **move** with the music;

   • **communicate** the joy of this arrangement in your face!

Reflecting - Evaluating

You have been learning how to use your singing voice, you have been developing your music reading and counting skills, and you have been studying David Elliott's *Jingle Bell Swing*. In rehearsal, you *produced* the song with your singing voice, you *practiced* the musicianship required to meet the musical challenges, and you *performed* in class or concert. As you review your performance, complete the following reflections for your journal.

1. **Describe** how you used your voice to perform this song.

2. **Describe** your ability to meet the musical challenges in performing artistically.

3. **Describe** how you could improve your performance.

   • As an assessment alternative, you may complete the Self-Evaluation or Concert Critique form to include in your *We Will Sing!* Performance Portfolio.

To improve your musicianship and to perform artistically, you may return to any of the problem-solving exercises as often as you like. It is also recommended that you review the related activities in Practice Project Six, p. 64-65.

Selected Recordings

We Will Sing! cassette, side 2. Glen Ellyn Children's Chorus.

For another example of a jazz piece in five, listen to *Take Five,* performed by the Dave Brubeck Quartet on:

Time Out. The Dave Brubeck Quartet. Columbia CK 40585.

MY PERFORMANCE PORTFOLIO

Jingle Bell Swing

Name:_____ Date:_____

Self - Evaluation

1. **Describe** your performance of *Jingle Bell Swing.*

    a. **Explain** how you achieved the jazzy swing style.

2. **Explain** what you enjoyed most in the rehearsal and performance of this song.

3. **Compare** and **contrast** your performance of *Jingle Bell Swing* to the Glen Ellyn Children's Chorus recorded version.

4. **Review** your performance of *Jingle Bell Swing* on audio or video cassette. **Decide** what you like about your performance and what you would like to improve.

APPENDIX

Glossary

of Musical Terms

accidental - A sign used in music notation to alter a particular pitch, usually by a semitone. *See* FLAT SIGN; SHARP SIGN; NATURAL SIGN; KEY SIGNATURE.

articulation - In notation, and performance, the characteristics of attack and decay of sounds or groups of notes. Examples include the slur, *staccato,* and *legato* designations.

bar line - Vertical lines inserted in a staff that organize notes into measures (see pg. 44).

bass clef - A symbol placed on the staff used in notating pitches sounding below middle C. The dots of the bass clef indicate the position of F below middle C. For singers, this clef is used to notate pitches associated with the changed male voice (see pg. 44).

binary - A two-part form found in tonal music. The first part generally modulates from the tonic to a related key. The second generally is a mirror of the first, modulating from the related key back to the tonic.

canon - A form of polyphony in which performers sing or play the same melody, but begin at different times. Examples in the text include *O Music, Sweet Music* and *Jubilate Deo.*

chromatic alteration - Changing a pitch with an accidental.

coda - In tonal music, a concluding section that functions as an appendage to the body of the form of the work. Codas may be either a few chords or notes, to many measures.

compound meter - A meter where the basic pulse is subdivided by three (i.e. $^6_8$, $^9_8$, or $^{12}_8$).

conjunct motion - A series of pitches that move by step (whole or half) rather than by leap.

crescendo - A dynamic marking indicating a change from a softer or quieter tone to a stronger or louder tone (see pg. 44).

decrescendo - A dynamic marking indicating a change from a louder or stronger tone to a softer or quieter tone (see pg. 44).

diphthong - A complex vowel sound in which the first half of the vowel formation continues into the second half of the vowel (see examples on pg. 35).

disjunct motion - A series of different pitches that move by leap rather than by step.

duple meter - A specific grouping of rhythms relaying an underlying pulse of two beats per measure (i.e. $^2_4$ or $^6_8$). *See* METER.

dynamics - The degree of intensity or volume of sound at which music is performed; from barely audible to the very fullest tone. The degree of volume is relative rather than absolute. (Refer to Practice Project Five for more detail.)

flat sign - (♭) A musical symbol used to lower a note by a semitone (or half-step) from its natural pitch.

free meter - In contrast to metered music, music in free meter consists of consecutive measures where no meter is specified. The rhythmic composition of each measure may vary widely.

half-step - A distance between two pitches; notes separated by a half-step are one semi-tone apart.

hexachord - The first six notes of a major scale. (*do - re - mi - fa - so - la*)

instrumental line - The staff, staves, or systems notated in a score that are played by one or more instrumentalists.

interval - The distance between two pitches. Note names (diatonic scale degrees) are counted from lowest to highest pitch. (See pages 81 - 82 for a list of perfect, major and minor intervals.)

key signature - A musical figure consisting of sharps or flats that occurs at the beginning of each staff indicating the tonality, or key of the piece. Each key has one central note called the "tonic" (called *do* in tonic solfa). (Refer to Practice Project Seven for more detail.)

legato - A type of articulation; notes performed legato have little perceptible separation. They are notated with either a long dash over (or under) the written note, or by the use of a slur to group several or many notes together.

major scale - A series of seven consecutive pitches following the pattern of intervals : whole-step, whole-step, half-step, whole-step, whole-step, whole-step, half-step. In tonic solfa, the major scale is *do* to *do'* (see pg. 73).

measure - The space between bar lines. It usually consists of a fixed set of durations of a particular type (see pg. 44). See METER SIGNATURE and RHYTHM for specific information regarding the arrangement of the notes.

melody - A coherent succession of musical pitches. In a broad and general sense, melody is the single line musical tune, while harmony accompanies it with simultaneous pitches.

meter - A steady grouping of rhythms relaying a pulse or beat, organized into strong and weak beats. The two principal kinds are duple meter (in patterns of 2's) and triple meter (in patterns of 3's). *See also* COMPOUND METER.

meter signature - The numerical indication in the score which denotes the meter of the piece. Meter signatures resemble fractions, where the "numerator" indicates the number of "denominator" note values contained in one musical measure. (e.g. $\frac{2}{4}$ where there are "2" quarter notes per measure.)

metric counting system - The use of number to delineate the beats and their subdivisions in a measure (i.e. 1 & 2 & 3 & 4 &) Also called METRIC SYLLABLES.

minor scale - A series of seven consecutive pitches; the natural minor scale follows the interval pattern whole-step, half-step, whole-step, whole-step, half-step, whole-step, whole-step. In tonic solfa, the natural minor scale is la, to la (see pg. 78).

musical instrument - A device producing sounds considered musical by the player. The sound is a result of vibrations produced by methods from four basic categories: by the basic material itself, by a stretched membrane, by a string with a soundboard, or by an air column vibrating in a cylindrical or conical tube.

musicianship - An non-verbal form of knowledge which enables a human to perform music; the knowledge is demonstrated through performance.

notation - A system of writing down music which specifies pitch, duration (including rhythm), timbre, and dynamic level or loudness. Modern notation consists mainly of symbols representing notes and rests written on what is known as the staff. Specific notes and rests and their relation to one another are outlined below.

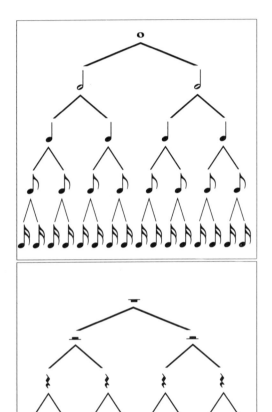

natural sign - (♮) A musical symbol modifying a particular note to be sounded at its natural pitch. It overrides any previous sharps or flats either indicated within the key signature or in the measure of occurrence. The validity of the sign lasts a) for the remainder of the measure, or within a single measure, b) until another sharp or flat sign occurs

octave - The interval between two pitches with the same name (i.e. middle C to C' or do to do').

performance portfolio - A record of musical growth and development kept by the student.

performance practice - The conventions and practice surrounding a piece of music that must be applied for an informed and accurate reading of the notation.

phrase mark - An arc showing a grouping of notes that form a section, often associated with a phrase of words in the text, much the way commas denote phrases in written language.

pitch - The high and low sounds of music. They are measured by fundamental frequency. Standard frequencies (measured in units called *Hertz*) are associated with music pitch, such as 256 Hz for middle C, and 440 Hz for a".

plainsong - Monophonic music consisting of one line without accompaniment, set to liturgical text. Vocal range is limited, and the text is sung in free rhythm.

rests - Symbols which represent musical silence. *See* RHYTHMIC NOTATION.

rhythm - In the most basic sense, the pattern of movement in time. Musical sounds occupy durations of time, and can be grouped together to form particular patterns. *See* METER and TEMPO.

rhythm syllables - Specific syllables which may be chanted or sung to perform rhythm patterns (i.e. *ta ta ti-ti ta* = ♩ ♩ ♫ ♩). (Refer to pg. 62 for a glossary of rhythm syllables.)

sharp sign - (♯) A musical symbol used to raise a note by a semitone (or half-step) from its natural pitch.

simple meter - A meter where the basic pulse is subdivided by two. Groupings can be duple (²⁄₄), triple (³⁄₄), or quadruple (⁴⁄₄).

singing voice - A musical way of vocalizing and articulating the pitched or rhythmic ideas of a song.

slur - A form of articulation; a curved line placed over a series of notes indicating that the grouping should be performed with no separation of sound; the slur can group either a large or small group of notes together, but contrary to the phrase mark, the slur is not usually associated to the text (see pg. 45).

speaking voice - The "everyday" use of the voice for communicating thoughts and feelings. It is different from the singing voice.

staccato - A form of articulation; a dot placed over or under a note indicating a detached sound of shortened duration; may be used in combination with other articulation marks for a variety of other sounds.

staff - A grouping of parallel lines and spaces on which notes are arranged. The staff in use today has been standardized to five lines and four spaces (see pg. 44).

syncopation - A shift in the pattern of emphasis by using rhythm patterns which shift the rhythm "off" the beat, or through the use of staccato or accent on beats that are normally weak.

system - Two or more staves played or sung simultaneously that occupy one line, read left or right, on the printed musical page. Staves are connected by vertical braces or bar lines.

tempo - The speed at which a musical work is performed.

ternary - A three-part form (ABA) found in tonal music. The first and third parts are either identical or closely related, beginning and ending in the tonic after modulating to a related key. the middle part is generally in the related key.

text - Words (often poetry or scripture) set to music in a song or vocal work.

tonality - The organized relationship of pitches around one central pitch (called "tonic"). Tonality embraces twelve major and twelve minor keys.

tonic solfa - A series of syllables used to represent specific pitches within a tonal scale. (e.g. *do - re - mi*)

treble clef - A symbol placed on the staff used to notate pitches sounding above middle C. The clef wraps around the second line of the staff to indicate the placement of G. For singers, this clef is used to notate pitches associated with the female voice, or the unchanged male voice (see pg. 41).

triple meter - A specific grouping of beats relaying an underlying pulse of three beats per measure (i.e. ¾ or ⅜). *See* METER.

triplet - Three notes of equal value written in the space normally occupied by two.

tutti - A direction in the score for the ensemble, or choir, to perform as a group, rather than a solo.

unison - 1. An interval (e.g. d to d'); 2. Voices singing or speaking the same material at the same time. *See also* CANON.

vocal line - The single staff, notated in a score of music, that is sung by a singer or choir.

whole-step - A distance between two pitches; notes separated by a whole-step are two half-steps or semi-tones apart.

Resources for the Teacher-Conductor

Selected Books

Bartle, Jean Ashworth. *Lifeline for Children's Choir Directors*. Toronto: Gordon V. Thompson, 1988.

Elliott, David J. *Music Matters: A New Philosophy of Music Education*. forthcoming.

Fowler, Charles, ed. *The Crane Symposium: Toward an Understanding of the Teaching and Learning of Music Performance*. Potsdam, NY: Potsdam College of the State University of New York.

Kemp, Helen. *Vocal Methods for the Children's Choir*. Philadelphia: Fortress Press, 1965.

Phillips, Kenneth. *Teaching Kids to Sing*. New York: MacMillan, 1992.

Pohjola, Erkki. *The Tapiola Sound*. Ft. Lauderdale, FL: Walton Music Corp, 1993.

Rao, Doreen. *Artistry in Music Education*. CME Library, Volume 1. New York: Boosey & Hawkes, 1987.

———. *The Artist in Every Child*. CME Library, Volume 2. New York: Boosey & Hawkes, 1988.

———. *The Art in Choral Music*. CME Library, Volume 3. New York: Boosey & Hawkes, 1990.

———. *Teaching Children Through Choral Music Experience*. CME Library, Volume 4. New York: Boosey & Hawkes, 1991.

———. *The Young Singing Voice*. 2nd ed. CME Library, Volume 5. New York: Boosey & Hawkes, 1987.

———. *Choral Music for Children: An Annotated List*. Reston, Virginia: Music Educators National Conference (MENC), 1990. (A single file copy library is available through AMC Music, Attn: Martha Palmer, 3330 Hilcroft, Suite H, Houston, TX 77057)

———. (co-author). *SING!* A choral music textbook for secondary school music. Houston: Hinshaw Music Textbook Division, 1987.

Szönyi, Erzsébet. *Kodály's Principles in Practice*. New York: Boosey & Hawkes, 1979.

Tacka, Philip, and Micheál Houlahan. *Sound Thinking. Musical Skill Development Through the Kodály Concept*. 2 vols. New York: Boosey & Hawkes, 1993.

Tacka, Philip, and Micheál Houlahan. *Sound Thinking. Music for Sight-Singing and Ear Training*. 2 vols. New York: Boosey & Hawkes, 1990.

Selected Journals and Articles

Elliott, David, J. "When I Sing: The Nature and Value of Choral Music Education." *Choral Journal,* March, 1993, Vol. 33, No. 8.

Rao, Doreen and David Elliott. "Musical Performance and Music Education." *Design for Arts in Education,* May/June 1990, Vol. 91, No. 5.

Rao, Doreen (guest editor). *Choral Journal* Special Issue on the Children's Choir. March, 1989, Vol. 29, No. 8. (Available through the American Choral Director's Association National Headquarters, P.O. Box 6310, Lawton, Oklahoma, 73506-0130, USA).

———. "Choral Singing and American Music Education Today." *International Choral Bulletin,* April, 1993.

———. "Selected Repertoire for Children's Chorus and Orchestra." *Research Memorandum Series,* 142, The American Choral Foundation, August, 1986.

———. "Children's Treble Voices: Interview with Sir David Willcocks." *Choral Journal,* March, 1985.

———. "Extended Choral Works for Treble Voices." *Choral Journal,* December, 1982.

Tagg, Barbara and Linda Ferriera (guest editors). *Choral Journal* Special Issue on the Children's Choir. March, 1993, Vol. 33, No. 8. (Available through the American Choral Director's Association National Headquarters, P.O. Box 6310, Lawton, Oklahoma, 73506-0130, USA).

Selected Video

On Location with Doreen Rao and the Glen Ellyn Children's Chorus. American Choral Director's Association (ACDA) *On Location* Series, Volume 1, 1987. (Available through the American Choral Director's Association National Headquarters, P.O. Box 6310, Lawton, Oklahoma, 73506-0130, USA)